Best of luck
it has been a pleasure knowing you.
Chrys

All the Best
17 Dud

Illwood RN

Discovery [...]ks in Warwickshire

Geoff
Walk Heaven to Everest
But your the tops

Geoff is there a link
to Andrew Miller?
Dave Clesh.

Enjoy your walk.
Remember Kenilworth

Dennis Kelsall

Good luck and God Bless
All the very best
Geoff Redfern
J Lambert

No more middle watches
All the breast
Pedlar Palmer.

Best wishes
Vera Gordon Banks

Best Wishes
John Large.

Heres to the next 42 yrs
Bob Pinfield

SIGMA Leisure

Published by Sigma Leisure – an imprint of
Sigma Press, 1 South Oak Lane, Wilmslow, Cheshire SK9 6AR, England.

British Library Cataloguing in Publication Data
A CIP record for this book is available from the British Library.

ISBN: 1-85058-580-6

Typesetting and Design by: Sigma Press, Wilmslow, Cheshire.

Cover photographs: top left – lychgate at Long Compton church; bottom left – thatched cottage at Ashorne; right – in the fields above Ilmington

Maps and photographs: the author

Printed by: MFP Design and Print

Acknowledgements

My warmest gratitude is due to the many people of Warwickshire, too numerous to recognise individually, who gave me unstinted help and hospitality in their eagerness to share the pleasures, history and stories of their beautiful countryside and its villages. I much appreciate their kindness, interest and enthusiasm. I am also grateful for the practical help and suggestions of Philip Round of the Ordnance Survey and Mike Overbeke and Stuart Ikeringill of Warwickshire County Council. Their collective assistance has been invaluable in determining viable routes and helping to ensure that walkers can actually use and enjoy the paths depicted on the maps. Finally, but not least, I wish to thank my wife Jan, whose untiring support, creative suggestions and countless contributions to the research and revision of the text were essential ingredients.

Dennis Kelsall

Contents

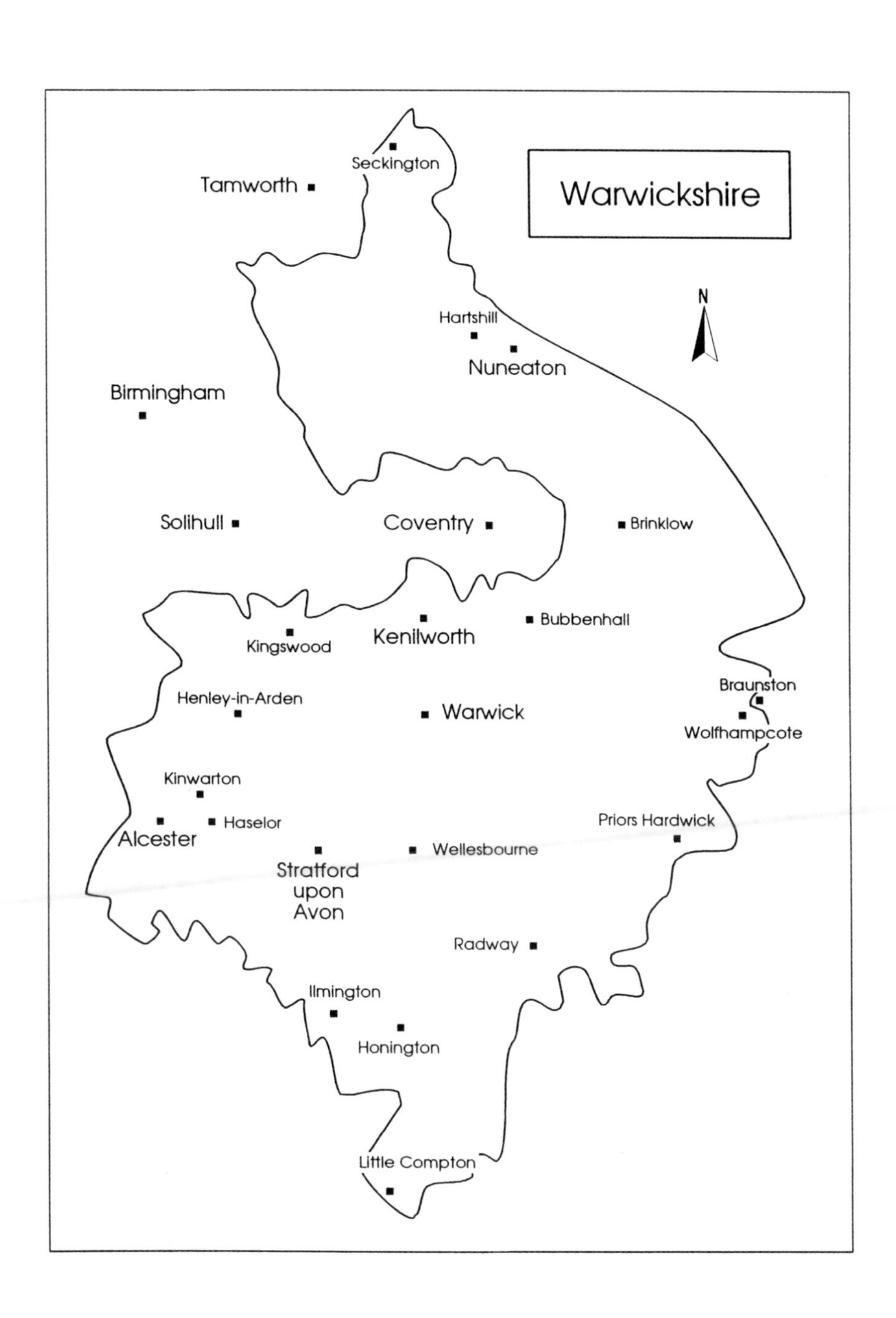
Warwickshire
N
Seckington
Tamworth
Hartshill
Nuneaton
Birmingham
Solihull
Coventry
Brinklow
Bubbenhall
Kingswood
Kenilworth
Henley-in-Arden
Warwick
Braunston
Wolfhampcote
Kinwarton
Haselor
Alcester
Priors Hardwick
Wellesbourne
Stratford
upon
Avon
Radway
Ilmington
Honington
Little Compton

Key To Sketch Maps

Described Route

Road

Track

Motorway

Railway

Canal

Natural Watercourse

Churches

Other Buildings

Introduction

Surrounded by seven counties and about as remote from the sea as one can be in this country, few would dispute Warwickshire's claim to be the 'Heart of England'. Even before chronicles were kept, people, trade and ideas passed through it in their passage across the country and, over time, it has been a hub for every aspect of life; farming, industry, commerce and culture, with a rich pageant being played upon its stage. The landscape, shaped by nature, worked by man and infused with history has come to be regarded as one of the most 'English' of counties.

In parts, the topography is gently undulating. Higher regions lie to the north on the midland plateau and in a line of hills and escarpments on the county's southern and eastern boundaries, which is part of a sickle-shaped uplift extending from Dorset to Yorkshire. Elsewhere, expansive plains are drained in opposite directions by the Rivers Tame and Avon, whose many meandering tributaries reach out as tendrils across the countryside exploiting its every declivity. The ancient Forest of Arden once covered the north-western part, an area of woodland and heath that was gradually cleared and settled during medieval times. Now, it has all but gone, but a few small woods can show a continuity of sylvan management that have produced timber for building, manufacture and firewood since antiquity. Primeval forests also once extended across the south of the county but this had been long cleared in favour of agriculture before the Norman Conquest. Indeed, its name, Feldon, describes an open cleared land where, during the Middle Ages, large tracts were profitably turned over to wool production. The central region of the Avon Valley has always been rich growing country, and the tradition of orchards and market gardening extends from the Vale of Evesham.

Although there are no dramatic panoramas, soaring peaks or winding gorges, the county has a quiet beauty. To wander through it is to experience a subtly changing perspective, where distant views are replaced by more intimate scenes, copses and woods thin to sporadic hedgerow trees and arable fields succeed meadows, still bearing the marks of feudal cultivation. The varying colour of the soil underfoot portrays a journey through geological time, repeated in the many hues and textures of the stone used in the local buildings. Elsewhere, cottages in vernacular brick or of timber-frame portray the availability of other materials. Each place has its own individual character, a product of the many elements that formed it.

Since the boundary reorganisations of 1974, in which Birmingham and Coventry were encompassed within the new county of West Midlands, the county has few expansive industrial centres or even large towns. Most of its former quarries and mines have either been worked out or are no longer economically viable and it is surprising how quickly these areas that have suffered such intense exploitation can re-assume a verdant cloak. Today's commercial activity is generally on a small scale or within service industries, and the landscape, for the most part, portrays a rural quality that belies the intensity of a modern farming business.

Yet, industry has had as much historical significance in creating the countryside as agricultural and sociological influences. The introduction of the factory system concentrated the manufacture of such things as small metal goods, cloth, hats, gloves and much more, which had previously been dispersed throughout villages as cottage industries. People migrated to the towns, attracted by the prospect of employment and housing or driven by the fundamental changes to village life and society that enclosure, mechanisation and growing world trade wrought on agricultural practice. Village populations dropped during the later eighteenth and early nineteenth centuries and it is only greater affluence and increased personal mobility that has reversed that trend over the last decades.

Alongside that industrial legacy lies a history of transport. Ancient tracks, Roman roads and later routes can all be traced, but by the eighteenth century, their condition had deteriorated so appallingly that they barely sufficed to serve village economies. The eighteenth-century introduction of turnpikes was a significant advancement in reducing journey times and bettering safety and comfort for travellers, but a reliance on cumbersome horse drawn vehicles meant little improvement where the mass transport of goods was concerned. This remained both arduous and expensive and, without the development of canals and subsequently the railways, the Industrial Revolution could never have taken place.

Their pioneering eras have now gone and it is ironic that our own age relies once again upon roads. Many of the old thoroughfares lie underneath modern tarmac, but a few remain to be enjoyed as tracks and paths across open countryside. Some former railway lines are evident only as abandoned embankments and cuttings, but the canals have largely avoided a similar fate and are still plied by brightly coloured narrowboats, sailing through the fields. These former arteries of industry and communication often now sustain many wildlife refuges, splendid with a diversity of plant, insect and animal life.

Particularly rich are the canal banks and fringes of woodland, where throughout the year a succession of flowers and other plants mark the seasons. Hedgerows too gather flowers at their base and a variety of shrubs and bushes, often interspersed with trees, combine to make these living walls that divide the land. Set-aside policies and a more sensitive approach to the natural order of things have resulted in more native habitats developing amongst an otherwise heavily farmed landscape. Wider field margins, fallow corners and uncultivated islands are allowing wild flowers and plants to re-establish. In turn, these are encouraging the return of more insects and birds and will hopefully reverse some bleaker trends of the recent past. With the exception of the ubiquitous rabbit, mammalian wildlife is more secretive, but with luck and patience, there is much to see. Badgers and foxes abound as do the smaller creatures such as rodents and moles, who might be spotted scurrying in the litter of the undergrowth.

It is the memory of Warwickshire's most famous son, William Shakespeare, that each year draws countless pilgrims from across the world to Stratford in search of that quintessence of English civilisation that he has come to symbolise. Almost as popular is that most perfect of castles at Warwick and the romantic ruins of Kenilworth. Yet how few leave these well beaten trails to search out the land from which the poet drew his inspiration or explore the countryside on which the wealth to support the Elizabethan landowning classes was founded. It is beyond the narrow horizons of the tourist that the real Warwickshire is to be found, in its ordinary towns, quiet villages, country churches, grand houses and rural cottages. The story of its past is writ everywhere and, only by walking amongst it, will you fully appreciate what this historic county has to offer.

This short book of walks takes you through some of that diversity and encourages you to pause along the way to examine and reflect on both the obvious and less apparent works of nature and of man. The ever-changing seasons and the perpetual hands of natural and human progress will continually alter what is there and thus there is always something new to enjoy. Each walk has something different and there are features to suit every interest, a few places may be familiar, but others are less well known and will hopefully serve to inspire you in your own search for pastures anew.

The Practicalities

The walks have been chosen to represent different aspects of the county and are geographically scattered within its confines. All the routes are circular and connect villages or other places of interest where you are encouraged to spend time. They are of varying lengths and none should prove over-taxing. No indication of the time required to complete each has been suggested since this will be largely governed by individual capability, inclination and the amount of time spent in 'exploration' along the way. The longer walks incorporate a described 'cut through', enabling them to be considered as shorter walks, thus allowing greater time to be spent en route.

In general, the instructions are confined to the ongoing route and you are left to explore individual villages in your own way. There is much to see and a narrative description provides some background and history as to what is there, although it makes no pretence at being comprehensive. The majority of village churches are open during the day and you are invited to visit them freely. They would appreciate a donation towards their upkeep and many have postcards or pamphlets for sale providing a fuller account of their history than is possible in this small volume. Remember that they are places of worship and conduct your behaviour accordingly. Elsewhere are mentioned houses and gardens that are open to the public. Opening times vary and you are advised to enquire in advance as to their arrangements and admission prices. The majority of other houses and cottages are, however, private homes and farms and you are reminded to respect the owner's privacy and not wander from defined rights of way.

Wherever possible, footpaths, tracks and canal towpaths have been chosen in preference to roads, but their unavoidable occasional use does not detract from the pleasure of these walks. All the paths described were found to be passable when researching the volume, although inevitably standards vary. With under-use, stretches become a little overgrown, occasionally stiles and plank ditch-crossings collapse with age and the changing seasons and weather both make their mark. The County Council's Footpath Team is active in both keeping open and promoting the public footpath network and would welcome information regarding any problems you might encounter. Although not every footpath is signed, you should encounter no great difficulty in navigating across the countryside and, whilst a compass is not essential, it may sometimes prove helpful. Small sketch plans accompanying the walks are for guidance and are not intended to replace the definitive detail shown on Ordnance Survey maps, the relevant sheet number(s) of which are shown against each walk. The 1:50,000 Landranger series will prove adequate in supporting these walks, but the extra information given by the 1:25,000 Pathfinder series, particularly with regard to the positions of field boundaries, will prove indispensable in planning your own routes.

You should remember that, although you may be walking along public footpaths, the land is privately owned and in most cases, represents a farming livelihood. The vast majority of farmers and landowners welcome responsible walkers who respect the countryside and its life and work. To ensure that the good relationships that have been established are maintained you should follow a few basic rules and courtesies:

* Remain on public paths and tracks
* Use stiles and gates to cross fences, hedges and walls
* Close gates behind you
* Keep all dogs under strict control, particularly near livestock and at lambing time
* Do not interfere with or damage crops, buildings or equipment
* Guard against the risk of fire
* Take all litter home
* Protect wildlife, plants and trees, remember, it is an offence to pick many wild flowers

What to wear is largely a matter of choice and will depend upon the time of year and prevailing weather. Specialised equipment is not necessary but the advantages of comfortable and waterproof walking shoes and effective rainwear are readily apparent. Warm clothing in winter is an obvious requirement, but even in summer you can become uncomfortably chilled by a cool breeze and it is wise to carry a sweater. Warm summer days tempt 'T' shirts and shorts, but even relatively short exposure to the sun can cause burning and over-growing brambles or nettles have an affinity for unprotected legs. More sensible is a light shirt and slacks and a sun hat is often useful. If you intend to visit any buildings, muddy boots will not be appreciated, but a pair of sandles or light trainers can be easily carried in your day-bag. A lightweight pair of binoculars and a good field-guide to help in identifying birds and plants are also useful.

There is the opportunity to leave cars at or near the recommended starts of each walk, although not necessarily on a formal car park. You should park considerately and safely, without causing obstructions. For those using public transport, the standard of service is variable. Larger towns are served by national coach or rail and some villages are usefully covered by local buses. However, others receive merely a shopper service which is often impractical for the walker. A general indication of availability is given for each walk, but check timetables with operators. Again, the County Council can provide helpful information. If you want to stay a little longer, bed and breakfast facilities are plentiful during the summer months and beyond. On most walks, there are pubs or other refreshment close to the route, which are mentioned in the text. In summer and at weekends, the majority offer a snack lunch, although picnics are an equally good idea.

Having said all that, read on and choose tomorrow's walk to begin your own personal discovery of Warwickshire's lovely countryside.

Useful Information

Telephone Numbers

Warwickshire County Council – 01926 410410

Countryside Services – 0827 872660

Footpaths Officer (north) – 01926 412111

Footpaths Officer (south) – 01926 412987

Warwickshire Traveline – 01926 414140

Warwickshire Wildlife Trust – 01203 302912

British Waterways – 01564 784634

National Trust (Severn Region) – 01684 850051

Maps

The sheet numbers for the Ordnance Survey maps presently covering Warwickshire are as follows:

Landrangers: 139, 140, 150 and 151

Pathfinders: 893, 913, 914, 915, 934, 935, 936, 954, 955, 956, 975, 976, 977, 997, 998, 999, 1020, 1021, 1022, 1044 and 1068

Walk 1: Seckington, Shuttington, Austrey, No Man's Heath and Newton Regis

Warwickshire's countryside in the extreme north is open and rolling, with low undulating hills rising from the River Anker valley. The area has remained largely agricultural and been unaffected by coal mining just to the south. Expansive fields surround compact hilltop villages, the tall tapering spires of their churches standing as conspicuous features on the landscape. This fine walk explores something of these quiet, little visited villages and takes you by Warwickshire's most northerly 'castle'.

Although fairly lengthy, the route conveniently splits into two separate excursions and a suggested short-cut is described. The way is easily followed and, although some quiet lanes are incorporated, the majority is along field paths and tracks outside the villages.

Maps: Pathfinder: 893 or Landranger: 140

Start: Layby beside the B5493 immediately north of Seckington (Map Reference SK 260 076)

Transport: The most frequent services run from Tamworth to Shuttington, Austrey and Newton Regis.

Distance: 10½ miles or two walks of 5¾ and (from Newton Regis) 6¾ miles

Refreshment: Pubs lie on or near the route at Shuttington, Austrey, No Man's Heath and Newton Regis.

Head a few metres west from the layby to a discrete stile in the hedge in the left. In the centre of the meadow beyond, rise impressive earthworks of a Norman motte and bailey castle. They are skirted on the left by a grass trod, which runs beyond to a gate at the bottom of the field.

An outcrop of sandstone raises this spot prominently above the surrounding landscape, which has undoubtedly been the determining factor in attracting settlement here. Although Seckington is now little more than a hamlet, the grassy earthworks of the motte and bailey and its proud little church point to an earlier importance. Further evidence comes from its name, which derives from its possession by some long-forgotten overlord, Secca.

Once the scene of conspiracy, it was here that the Mercian king, Ethelbald, was murdered. His history is obscure, but it appears that he spent a number of years as a fugitive after his ascendancy was usurped before finally being able to assume his throne in 716. He gained a reputation for fierce courage and leadership and extended the Mercian kingdom throughout the area south of the Humber and into Wales. Although an effective administrator who gave some support to the early Christian church, his rule was often harsh and he engendered criticism from the church and opposition within his own ranks. Ethelbald's position was eventually challenged in 752 in an uprising led by Cuthred and he was ultimately defeated in battle at Burford. Ethelbald retired to Seckington with his remaining adherents who, now disillusioned, possibly also saw their

Ivy cladding a Georgian farmhouse in Seckington

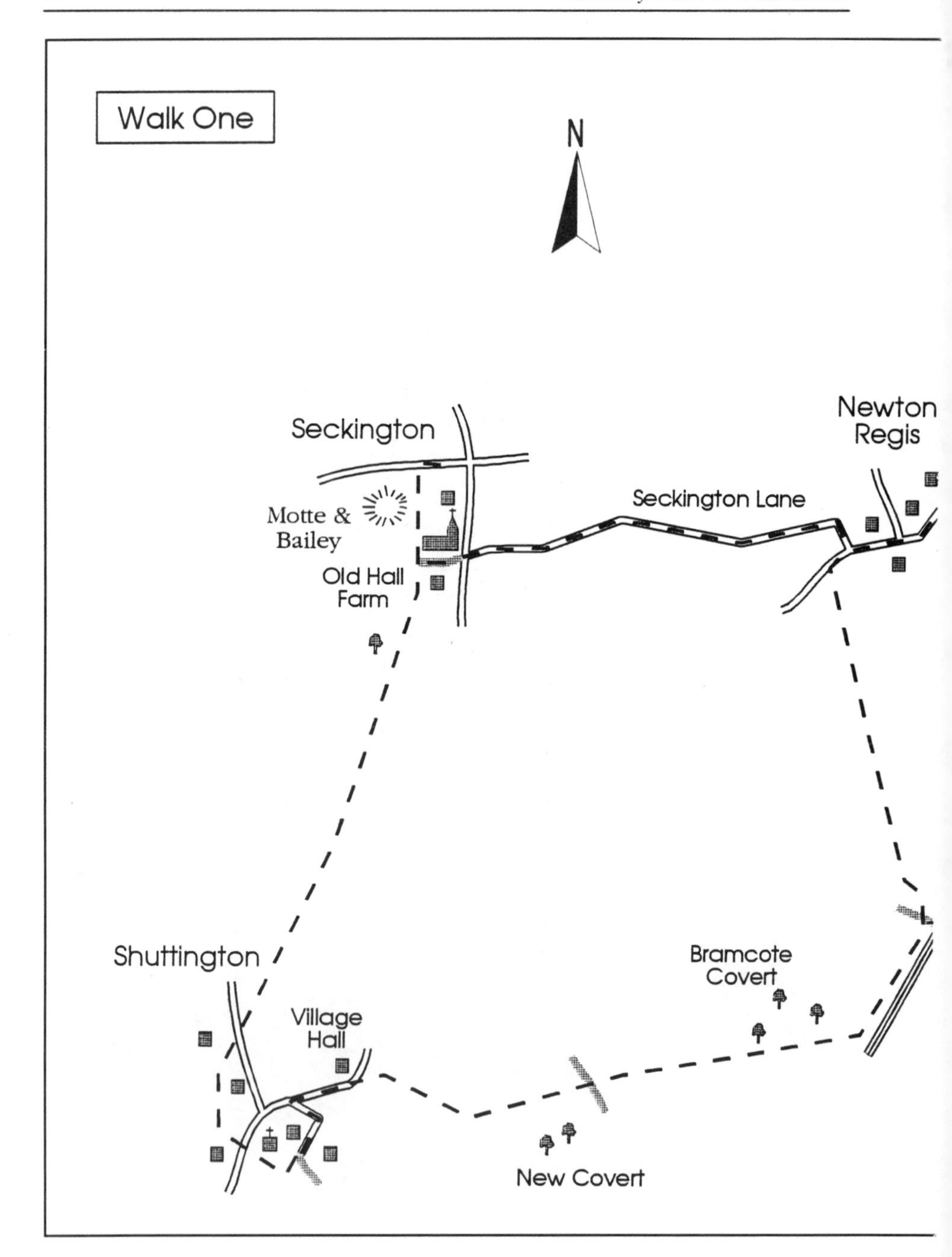

Walk One
N
Seckington
Newton
Regis
Seckington Lane
Motte &
Bailey
Old Hall
Farm
Shuttington
Village
Hall
Bramcote
Covert
New Covert

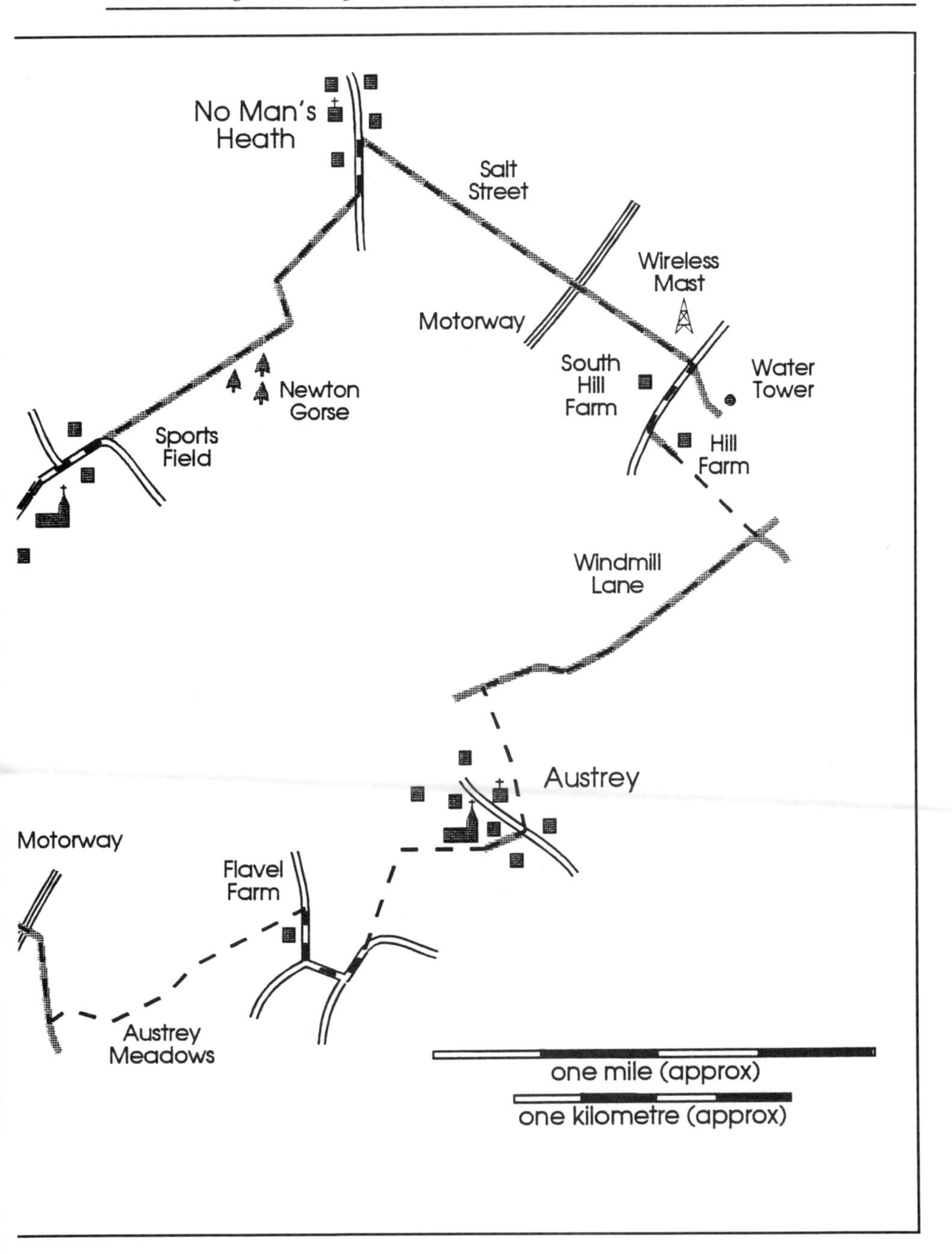
No Man's Heath
Salt Street
Wireless Mast
Motorway
South Hill Farm
Water Tower
Newton Gorse
Sports Field
Hill Farm
Windmill Lane
Austrey
Motorway
Flavel Farm
Austrey Meadows
one mile (approx)
one kilometre (approx)

own position compromised. Five years later, the king was killed whilst he slept, the deed being attributed to Beornred who ruled for a short period after his death.

The earthworks of the 'castle' are attributed to the Normans and remain an impressive monument. Strategically sited to make the best use of the topography, a steep central mound still stands 30 feet high, enclosed within an encircling fosse and embankment. All traces of its wooden palisades and buildings have long since gone, replaced by a mantle of shrubs and trees and populated only by nuzzling sheep.

Through the gate, walk down the next field and, passing left of an ash tree, join a field track to another gate at the bottom. Beyond, turn half-right and cross the next two fields heading towards a building on the skyline that resolves into a byre and yard as you approach. Pass through a gate to its right and, maintaining the same direction as before, make for a gate in the middle of the far hedge. Go through into the next field and again cross diagonally to a stile in the middle of its bottom hedge. Once over, walk up the field beside a hedge on the left towards some houses at Shuttington, the path ending at a lane on the edge of the village. Cross over and follow a hedged track beside the houses. At its end, climb a stile to a field and carry on a few metres to then pass through a gap to another field on the left. Head diagonally to a stile about half way along its opposite boundary and walk on, emerging onto a small housing estate. Keep going across the central green to the main road beyond. Cross to Church Lane opposite, a short track terminating at a kissing-gate into St Matthew's churchyard.

Perched atop a hillside from which there are extensive views, Shuttington is an ancient place, its manor with an attendant corn mill being mentioned in the Domesday survey. Immediately to the south lie the extensive Warwickshire coal-fields, whose exploitation has left its mark upon the landscape, not least in the mountain of spoil visible to the south-east. The workings around Alvecote were first developed in 1848 and became a valuable resource during the war years. However, they were continually beset by seepage from the river and production ended in 1965 when it became uneconomic to continue their drainage, despite the course of the river being diverted. Empty workings and the depressions left by subsidence quickly flooded to form the lakes you now see, which have since attracted a considerable waterfowl population. They are a designated nature reserve and SSSI managed by Warwickshire Wildlife Trust.

Beside the lakes, the Coventry Canal and railway line take advantage of the river's level bed, all seemingly jostling for position to elicit the most favourable route along the valley. It took over twenty years to cut the canal from Coventry to Fradley, partly because Brindley, the original engineer, was sacked for being involved in too many other projects. The waterway, primarily built to carry coal from the mines, was finally opened in 1790 with the railway, linking Stafford and Rugby, following 84 years later.

In 1159, a Benedictine house was founded beside the Anker at Alvecote and Shuttington manor was given as an endowment. Very little remains of the priory, although a finely carved Norman doorway and a low square dovecote still stand in a secluded area beside the canal. It appears that the Prior did not always enjoy good relations with his neighbours as in 1221, Robert de Bramcote, whose manor lay a short distance upstream, complained of flooding caused by raising the weir of the mill pond to gain more water for the priory's mill. After the Dissolution in about 1535, Shuttington was given to Lord Audley, Henry VIII's Lord Chancellor, who was involved in the trials of both Anne Boleyn and Catherine Howard.

Seckington's tiny church of St Matthew is sadly kept locked, but has much of interest. Older than many in the area, it dates from 1150, with the evidence of haphazard stonework in its walls showing much alteration over the ages. There was substantial rebuilding in the thirteenth century with further restorations in the nineteenth and early twentieth centuries. It is a pleasingly simple, squat building, built from orange-grey stone. Presiding over the western end of its tiled roof, is an unusual diminutive wooden belfry, capped in green copper and topped by a weather cock. The surrounds of the western door show weathered carving, said to have been brought from nearby Alvecote Priory. An open graveyard surrounds the church and contains the eighteenth-century grave of Thomas Spooner, who was claimed the heaviest man in England at some 40 stone.

Go through a gate beyond the church and along a short gravel path between houses to a road. Turn left and, skirting the perimeter of a small housing estate, walk to a junction at its end. There, to the right, a lane leads from the village. Where it shortly bends by the village hall, take a way-marked field track on the right. Keep going beyond its end, following a hedge on the left until it turns a corner. There, bear right over the field to a lane bordering its far hedge. Enter another field through a gap opposite and walk ahead to its far side. There, turn left and follow a hedge to its corner, crossing a plank bridge into the next field. Keep on beside a small copse, eventually emerging through a rather overgrown gap onto a farm track.

Cross over, the onward Right of Way following the field hedge on its left side away from the track. (If it remains overgrown, it might be avoided by following the hedge on the right.) Where the hedge later bends left near a small overgrown pool, turn to the right through it and walk across the field, taking the right-hand edge of a distant copse, Bramcote Covert, as your sight mark. Keeping the same line, cut the corner of the next field to its bottom hedge, there crossing a ditch into a large open field. Walk on, still towards the edge of the wood, continuing beyond it to the bottom corner of the field by the motorway, where a stile and culvert lead into the adjacent field. Follow the perimeter beside the motorway towards a bridge and climb its embankment to a crossing farm track.

At this point, you can shorten the walk by going across country towards Newton Regis. In which case, turn left away from the bridge, but immediately fork right to follow a wooden fence down the opposite side of the embankment. At the bottom, cross to a clump of trees on the opposite side of the field and walk through to emerge over a plank bridge into the field beyond. Turn right and walk to its corner and, over a stile, keep going beside the continuing perimeter hedge. A little further on, the hedge strikes off to the right, but maintain your direction across the field to a gap in the far corner. Keep going for a few metres, the hedge now on your left, but then pass through a gap into the adjoining field and follow the hedge on its opposite side to a stile in the corner. Beyond, there is a short enclosed path bordering an overgrown field to another stile. Over, walk with the hedge on your left along the edge of a succession of fields, climbing a last stile to a lane west of Newton Regis. Turn right, and then left into Seckington Lane, which returns you to Seckington Village.

The main walk crosses the bridge and after reverting to field level, continues as a field track. A short distance on, just after a culverted stream, go left at the end of a hedge and walk across the bottoms of a succession of long fields. The exits from some are not obvious and pass through the hedge to the right of the corner.

These fields, known as Austrey Meadows, would at one time have been regularly flooded by winter rains, draining to provide rich summer grazing for cattle. Such lush meadows were an important element of the pre-enclosure communal farming practices, each inhabitant of the village having rights to graze a number of animals depending upon the terms of his tenure. The lack of over-intensive cultivation has left considerable variety in their plant life, particularly in the fringes that border the secluded stream winding amongst the trees and shrubs on the left.

Beyond the meadows, keep the same direction across the middle of a much larger field to an indented corner on its far side. Cross into a small meadow and walk on to a stile and gate in the far corner beside a house, Flavel Farm. Turn right at the lane beyond, following it a short distance to a junction. There, go left and after a left-hand bend, look for a waymark in the high hedge on the left. Cross a stile into a meadow and follow its left-hand hedge, passing into the next field through a gap. Keep going, the hedge now on the right, to a third field. A few metres on, the hedge bends right bringing Austrey church into view. Walk towards it, finally leaving through a kissing-gate into the churchyard.

The village, resting at the foot of a gently rising hill, has grown considerably in recent times, but attractive buildings and cottages remain from earlier periods including some timber-framed and vernacular brick cottages.

The parish church, dedicated to St Nicholas has a thirteenth-century tower, but the body of the building was rebuilt in the following century. The broach spire is characteristic of many Midland churches, in which the octagonal faces of the spire are melded to an un-parapeted square tower below by the addition of pyramidical buttresses. The building is a fine example of the well proportioned elegance of the Early English architectural style and inside, the clustered columns supporting the clerestory are a typical feature of the period. Behind the altar, there is a finely carved wooden screen bearing the tenets of the Christian faith on its panels. Also of interest is an Elizabethan oaken chest with four locks for which the keys would have been held by at least two people to ensure propriety over the funds. On the north wall are copies of manuscripts which give insight into matters of former importance to the village. One, a letter written in 1690. spares the parish from providing footsoldiers to the militia, the home guard of the day, on account of its remoteness within the county. Instead it had to furnish two equipped horsemen should the need arise. The second, from 1796, is an eleven year indenture putting a poor boy of the parish to learn the wool knitting trade. In return for relieving the parish of the responsibility of feeding the poor wretch, the master benefited from virtually free labour for the duration of his long apprenticeship.

Leave the churchyard by a gate at its eastern corner onto a lane and walk to its end.

The Bird in Hand at the bottom of Church Lane retains its thatched roof and outside stands a medieval cross. The octagonal stepped base is original and dates from the fifteenth century, although the cross itself is more recent, being erected in 1897 to commemorate the Diamond Jubilee of Queen Victoria.

Turn left and walk through the village towards the post office. Immediately after passing Kirtland Close, leave the road along a short track beside a white cottage on the right and climb the stile at its end. Turn left and follow a

hedged track behind the cottage, which ends behind the village's Baptist Chapel.

Better seen from the road, the chapel was built in 1819 for a congregation formed in 1808 and its design is a stark contrast to that of the church. The puritanical severity of its brick walls is emphasised by plain windows and its elevated site. Forming the wall of a small car park and fronting the chapel entrance are some beautifully incised headstones, cleft from Charnwood Forest's Swithland slate. Although here, a simple, yet perfect adornment, their crisp austere lines sometimes appear an anomaly when found amongst the age-mellowed stones of the old parish churches in the area. The Non-conformist tradition in the village can be traced back to at least 1672, when a house belonging to John Kendall was licensed for meetings by Presbyterians. A supposed descendant of his in 1845 married John Stolberg Stuart, Count d'Albanie, who claimed to be the grandson of Bonnie Prince Charlie.

Ignoring the gate ahead, cross the stile on your right into a meadow and follow its left boundary to a plank bridge and stile in the far corner. Walk ahead across the next field, mounting a stile into a third meadow. Keep going to a final stile in the far left corner onto a hedged track, Windmill Lane. Turn right and go up the hill.

A windmill used to stand on the top within a small triangular patch of ground hidden behind a tall hedge on the left. No trace remains, but it was possibly still in use in the eighteenth century.

Higher up the gradient eases and eventually, the bordering hedges end at a junction with a track entering from the right. There, go left on a grass path beside the hedge that leads to Hill Farm. Carry on through the farm yard and follow the ensuing track to the lane at the bottom. Turn right and walk up beyond South Hill Farm to find a track leaving on the left beside a transmitter mast. This, after shortly crossing the motorway, drops to a lane outside No Man's Heath.

The name Salt Street describes its former use. By the Middle Ages a considerable salt industry had grown up in the Droitwich area and, before the advent of serviceable roads or canals, packhorses transported the salt to markets around the country. This salt trail is thought to have been used as such until the 1880s. This track marks the boundary between Warwickshire and Leicestershire, which runs more or less in a straight line, apart from a kink to incorporate No Man's Heath, to the northernmost tip of the county, about a mile beyond. Before the local government reorganisations of 1974, No Man's Heath marked the juxtaposition of Warwickshire, Leicestershire, Derbyshire and Staffordshire. Derbyshire's boundary has been removed to the River Mease, just a little to the north. However, the Four Counties pub, alongside the main road just to the north, ignores these administrative diversions and has retained its original name.

No Man's Heath is a compact collection of tidy houses and a small brick chapel sat amid neatly maintained fields, and shows little of the wildness that its name evokes. Yet before 1863, this was open heath and, in a meadow to the south of what is now the village, there remain distinctive traces of open cultivation. The village developed from squatters settling on common lend and its remoteness from more civilising influences encouraged some of the more seamy leisure activities of the day such as cock fighting, bare knuckle boxing matches and horse racing. In the early part of the twentieth century, it was a lively place beside a main road with several shops and a bakery. One resident remembers circuses and fairs passing through to Ashby. These events were always an occasion, with everybody gathering to watch elephants and other exotic animals follow the slow lumbering vehicles and caravans being drawn by horse or steam through the village. On occasions the company rested awhile, since on Sunday, the procession was not allowed through Ashby until after church service had ended.

Go left along the lane for a short distance to the second of two adjacent field gates on the right beside a large ash tree. A track crosses the farmland to two barns and, after turning left and then right beyond them, leads to Newton Regis, emerging at the corner of Newton Lane beside the village

sports-field. Walk ahead past the school and then around by the church to the centre of the village.

Newton originally acquired its descriptive 'Regis' from its possession by Henry II, a king little loved by his subjects. Over the ensuing years, the village became known as Newton-in-the-Thistle and only reverted to Regis after Charles Stuart had briefly tarried to pray in the church before a battle at nearby Seckington. The manor is not mentioned in the Conqueror's survey, although a reference to some lands held by Juhell of William, son of Corbucion, may correspond with the area and suggests that the area was subordinate Seckington. Even in Henry II's time, the church was only a chapel to that at Seckington. Despite its modern houses, the village remains picturesque, with a comfortable mixture of rustic brick and black white timber-framed cottages, some of which still bear their thatch. Larger brick houses in the Georgian style overlook a delightful village pond, its surface brushed by the tendrils of weeping willows and populated by a family of ducks, eager to share in any picnic.

St Mary's Church stands isolated within an open raised churchyard. Of similar age to others in the area, it too carries a tapering spire, though here emerging from a crenellated tower. At its base in the north-west corner of the church is a 'squint hole', which allowed lepers or beggars observe the proceedings without mingling with the congregation. Fragments of early coloured glass decorate several of the windows and, on the splays of the north windows, are traces of fourteenth-century painted decoration. The walls of many churches were originally painted, either in patterns or with pictures that reinforced a virtuous life and warned of the penalties for sin. Also of interest are two stone slabs. One, of alabaster from the fifteenth century, bears a priest and child, its hands clasped in prayer at his feet. The other, an earlier coffin lid that was found buried in the chancel, has a carved relief, also of a priest.

Follow the road to the edge of the village and turn right into Seckington Lane,

along which Seckington lies about a mile away. At the end of the lane, cross over and go down The Green. It passes the entrance to Old Hall Farm, bending right to go between barns. Towards the far end, climb a short track and embankment on the right to a lane opposite the churchyard.

The parish church, dedicated to All Saints, stands peacefully surrounded by monuments to its former congregation, with a graceful spire rising from its tower. The oldest parts, dating from the thirteenth century, are to be found in the chancel, but much of the church was rebuilt or changed in the following century. Some glass from that time is incorporated in the window traceries. It was substantially restored in the nineteenth century, with works that included a rebuilding of the tower and spire. Notice the small low window on the south side of the chancel, another squint hole with the same function as that at Newton Regis. The present low screen separating the nave from the chancel is thought to be part of a fifteenth-century rood screen, whose presence is indicated by marks on the sides of the chancel arch. A painted alabaster monument is to Robert Burdett, who was a counsellor to Queen Elizabeth. He is depicted kneeling with his wife and children. Also of interest are two fourteenth-century effigies, one of a woman, wearing a wimple head-dress and the other, a priest with a cross, book and chalice.

Leave the churchyard through a gate at its north-western corner, turn right and go through a wooden gate into the field beyond. Retrace your steps past the castle to return to the layby on the main road.

Walk 2: Hartshill and Oldbury

From a cursory glance at the map, the walker may feel inclined to give this area a wide berth. Conurbation, industry, mining and quarrying are conspicuous and have shaped this area since the beginning of the industrial age and before. Yet, this walk has as much to offer the inquisitive walker as any in this short volume. The effects of industry, although often great, are sometimes relatively short lived and nature quickly moves back to reclaim her own. Proximity to industry sometimes means that land which might be intensively farmed or otherwise used is abandoned to a more natural state. This shorter walk, through woodland and open field, in searching out some of these corners of interest looks at other by-products of an earlier industrial age.

Maps: Pathfinder: 914 or Landranger: 140

Start: Visitor Centre at Hartshill Hayes Country Park (Map Reference SP 316 943)

Distance: 6¼ miles

Transport: The country park lies close to Hartshill which is well-served from Atherstone, Coventry and Birmingham.

Refreshment: Café at Country Park Visitor Centre

There are few places in Britain where rocks formed during the volcanic chaos of the earliest epochs are naturally revealed, but Hartshill is one. Known as the Nuneaton Inlier, the ridge of high ground that runs north-west from Nuneaton contains a remarkable series of volcanic, igneous and sedimentary rocks of the Pre-Cambrian and Cambrian eras formed between 600 to 410 million years ago. The ripples of orogenic activity have tilted and faulted its strata, bringing to the surface volcanic tuffs, limestones, quartzite and red, dark and green shales. Dolerite and localised deposits of metallic ores are also found, resulting from intrusions of molten salts and gases into layers of sedimentary rock. To the west, coal measures lie close to the surface, the legacy of a vast tropical

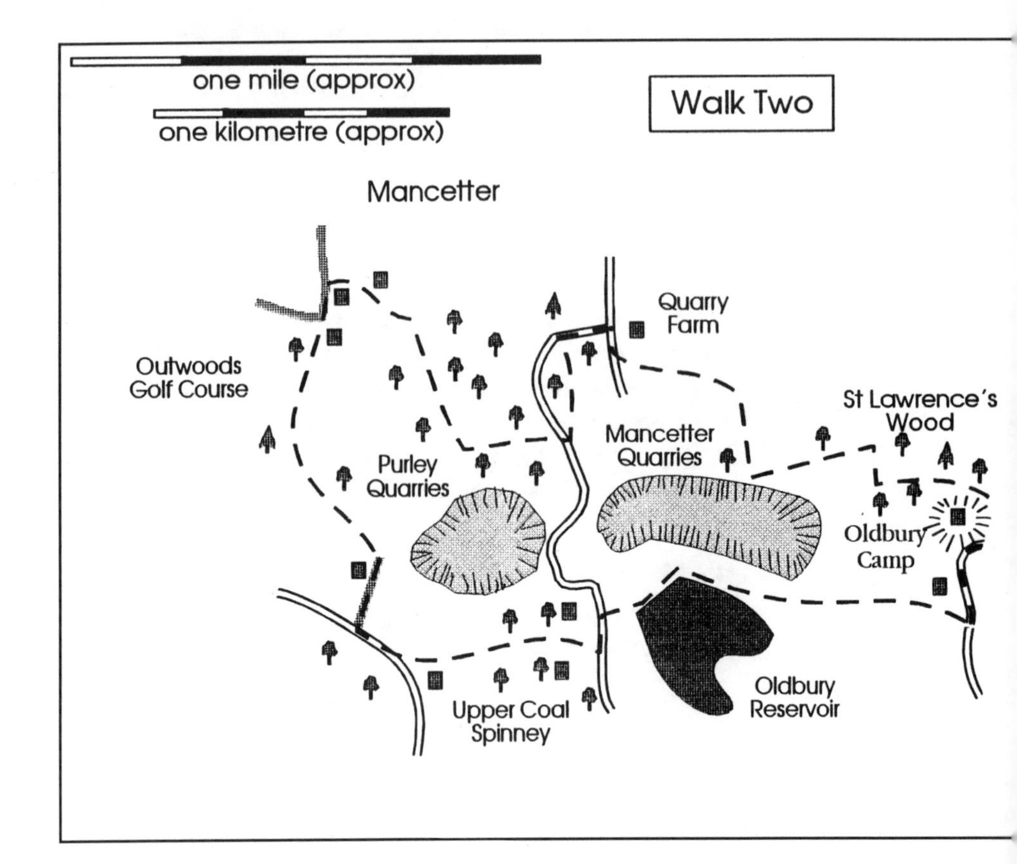

swamp that covered large areas of Britain during the Carboniferous period, some 285 to 210 million years ago. In contrast, alongside the ridge to the north-west, some of the youngest geological deposits can be found as flint-bearing glacial drift.

For more than 10,000 years, man has been attracted by the resources and position of this small hill. Finds of worked flints, scrapers and a hand axe indicate the presence of Early Stone Age hunter-gatherers, who followed the retreating ice in a gradually warming climate. From around 4000 BC, Late Stone Age farmers settled the higher ground, where it would have been easier to create

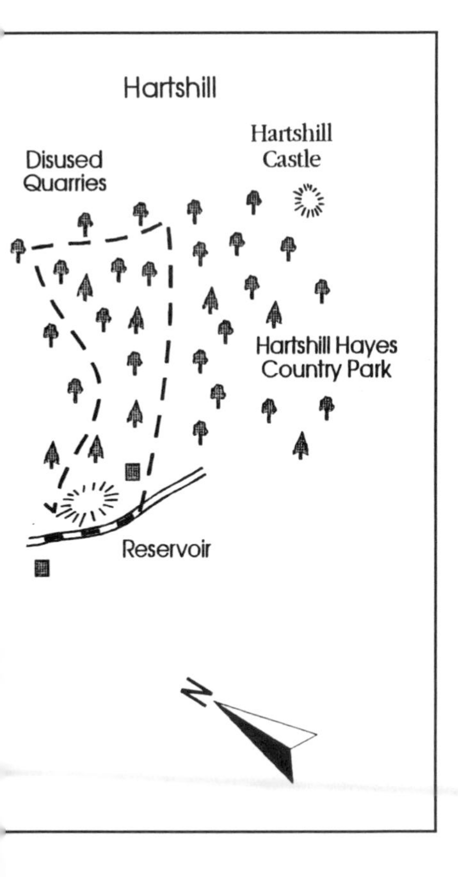

and maintain clearings within a pervasive woodland. A burial from about 2000 BC containing a later Bronze Age interment dated to circa 1400 BC, revealed burial urns and other pottery, stone and metal artifacts. Stone axes crafted from camptonite, an igneous rock unique to here, have been discovered as far away as Wiltshire, indicative of early trading patterns. More obvious is the legacy of an Iron Age community. Oldbury camp has been dated to about 700 BC and was one of several across the Midlands. The fort extended over seven acres and consisted of a hill-top enclosure defended by several outer ditches. Close by was a crossing of established routes, one from Cheshire to the east coast and the other from Wiltshire to the north east, which must have given importance to the place as a trading centre. The area also had its own resources in outcrops of iron ore further along the ridge, plentiful supplies of timber and an adjacent river.

The Romans arrived before 47 AD, and built a fort at Mancetter beside Watling Street, Romanising an older British trackway. There is evidence to suggest that the Briton's revolt, led by Boudicca, against the conquerors ended in a battle here in 60 AD. Finds of later pottery and traces of kilns, glass furnaces, coal mining and stone, copper and iron ore quarrying suggest an important area supporting a large established population. The Normans followed the Saxons, building a motte and bailey castle on the eastern edge of Hayes Wood. Throughout medieval times mining and quarrying continued, but it was the coming of the industrial age that perhaps wrought the greatest changes on the area, with intensive mineral extraction making irrevocable changes to the landscape.

Although the work still continues, the hard stone being in demand for road surfacing, nature is returning to claim her own, softening the harsh lines of industry with a rich cloak of vegetation. Mixed woodland and heathland vie with open grass and hedgerows, resulting in a diversity of flowers, shrubs and trees, which in turn provide habitats for all manner of wildlife. Butterflies dance amongst the flowers and numerous birds flutter between the hedges and woodland trees. At dusk you may see a badger and your nostrils will certainly tell you where a fox has crossed your path.

Leave the car park by the marked 'Hayes Wood' trail, which begins to the right of the information centre. Keep to the main path until you reach a gravel track and then follow it left to the next junction (marker post 3). At that point, take the path on the right dropping to a wooden bridge over a stream. Now, keep ahead until you reach the north-eastern edge of the wood, marked by a gate.

Although naturally forested in antiquity, today's woods are the product of formal management to provide timber for building, manufacture and even fuel, although coal is plentiful here. Woodland is managed in different ways to suit the type of tree and the purpose to which the wood will be put. Sometimes the prime growth is preserved and timber periodically harvested by coppicing or pollarding, dependent upon whether the poles or branches are taken from the base of the trunk or higher up. Alternatively, the full tree is felled and the wood left to regenerate naturally or, more often, be replanted. Hayes Wood has been managed for at least the last 250 years, first under the manorial estate and then in the successive ownership of the Coal Board, Forestry Commission and the County Council. Much of the mature hardwood has been harvested since the beginning of the twentieth century and replanted with larch and Scots pine. In turn this will be felled and the wood allowed to regenerate more naturally. Lime, oak, alder and ash are again becoming established to produce a more varied habitat for wildlife. Even a conserved woodland needs management since young trees become tall and leggy in competing for light and, without intervention, would weaken. Selective felling encourages a healthy growth and, in time, a balance of young and mature timber.

Don't go through the gate, instead, turn left on a path around the perimeter of the wood following the marshy valley downstream past the disused quarries. Take the right fork where the path splits, then cross a stream and again choose the track to the right, shortly coming to a stile. However, do not cross it but stay with the perimeter path.

In 1820, manganese ore was discovered at the eastern end of the wood. This was an essential ingredient in the manufacture of chlorine solution, used as a bleach in linen and cotton production. As only three other deposits of the ore were known in the country, Hartshill's deposit assumed the importance of a gold strike, but by 1860 the lode had been exhausted and the quarry was abandoned. A largely open grass site developed that favoured butterflies and some 26 species have been recorded here including the ringlet, its only recorded sighting in Warwickshire. The area, designated a SSSI, is now becoming more overgrown and reverting to woodland.

Stick with the perimeter path, ignoring tracks into the wood, until you reach a junction by a children's playground. Turn right, passing a stile, to reach another junction on the edge of the wood. Follow the track to the right across open meadow, to join a gravel path coming down from the left. Carry on towards St Lawrence's Wood, forking left at a marker.

The first high embankment on the left is a water reservoir and further on, above a wood, overgrown slopes mask the flanks of Oldbury Camp. Its encircling ramparts and ditches have largely disappeared, but the expert eye can still trace them through the wooded banks. Oldbury Hall, built about 1780, took advantage of the site's prominence, but that too has gone, demolished in 1950 after suffering a fire from an incendiary bomb in 1942. The site remains private ground and there is no access.

Shortly, the way drops steeply into a valley, joining another path at the bottom. Turn left and, at a hairpin bend, go ahead through a gap on a waymarked path.

St Lawrence's Wood takes its name from a small chapel that once stood nearby, built in the tenth century as an outpost to Polesworth Abbey. It housed a small community of nuns and the mineral rich waters of a nearby spring, St Lawrence's Well, were reputed to cure eye ailments. Much of the timber on the bank has recently been felled and replanted with a mixture of native trees. Now unfettered by a dark canopy, the undergrowth has assumed dominance and for a time, light loving plants and flowers will be able to grow freely.

A meadow opens ahead, the path rising on the right beside a hedge. Towards the top, it turns abruptly right, climbing over the hill and descending as a track to Quarry farm. Proceed beyond the farm buildings to a lane and go right to a junction.

From the top, the effect of massive stone-quarrying operations can be seen, but of far greater interest is the tremendous variety of plants growing in the hedgerows and meadows. For a number of years, much of this land has either not been intensively farmed or left largely fallow. As a result, many species, once commonplace in the farmland of a century ago, have become re-established and attracted a rich tapestry of bird and insect life. This section of the walk is a particular delight in spring and early summer.

Turn left and climb for about a third of a mile to a pull-in (much of the road walk can be avoided by using a parallel woodland path on the left). Just beyond, an unmarked footpath on the right leaves the road dropping gently into Purely Chase Wood.

The wood sustains a great variety of trees, including beech, birch, oak, sycamore and lime. Lime trees were specifically grown in the area to support the hat trade which had developed from a cottage industry. The timber was used to fashion blocks on which the felt was shaped into hats.

Losing height through the wood, the path eventually runs along the edge of

Purely Chase Wood

an open meadow to a slab bridge and stile at its northern point. Cross the meadow to a short climbing path on the other side, which ends at a dirt track beside a house. The Outwoods Golf Course lies to the left at the end of the track. Keep going past the club house and climb beside a hedge over a hill. Drop down at the far side of the course to pass through a gate onto a farm track.

Behind the course to the left lie the huge excavations and spoil tips of Purley Quarries. Flooding has created a long lake, its waters coloured a deep aquamarine by metallic ores seeping from the rock.

Walk to a road at its end and turn left. After a few metres, branch off through a gate beside a solitary house. A track drops through an extension of the golf course before passing through more woodland, Upper Coal Spinney, and eventually rises to a gate. The footpath lies over a stile on the left, carrying on to terminate at the road beside a large house. Turn left and, after about 100 metres, abandon it for an unmarked path on the right, dropping between cultivated fields into disused quarries and across the dam of an abandoned reservoir.

To the north-east runs the Coventry Canal. Fully opened in 1790, it allowed the mass transport of coal and stone to the growing industrial centres of the Midlands and the North. It derived some of its water from a stream here, originally known as Pool Meadow. The dam was constructed to enhance that supply and, until a few years ago, was an attraction for anglers, sailors and skiers. However, the water became acid, killing fish and affecting bathers. Underground seepage from flooded workings of an old coal mine near Slacks Farm, about a mile to the south, is thought to have caused the contamination. Lime was used in an unsuccessful attempt to neutralise it and eventually the water began to pollute the canal. Consequently, a few years ago the lake was drained and has not been used since. The surrounding area now appears quite abandoned, but vegetation is recolonising the banks and is creating new habitats.

Over the dam, turn right, and follow a meandering path through the scrub beside the dwindling lake.

Immediately to the east lie the quarry workings. The perimeter ground is unstable and the workings deep and sheer sided. Don't be tempted to explore and take particular care of young children and dogs.

Eventually, having crossed a stile, the path leaves the reservoir behind and curves to the left, climbing into a valley beside a former spoil heap rising on the left. Higher up, a gully develops in the centre of the valley, with the better path on the right.

The sense of desolation is quickly left behind and the area, unaffected by herbicides and pesticides, has become recolonised by a profusion of wild flowers and grasses.

Over a stile at the top, walk ahead across a small paddock and then along a short enclosed path to emerge through a high hedge onto a lane. Exercise caution here as there is no verge to the road. To the left, the lane bends below the site of Oldbury Camp and then shortly returns you to the car park. Alternatively, you can re-enter the country park just beyond Oldbury Grange and further explore the woods.

Walk 3: Brinklow and Easenhall

Beginning at Brinklow, this is a gentle walk that takes advantage of a delightful stretch of canal towpath to link a ramble through quiet countryside. The town itself is of interest, in the attractive assortment of buildings that line its wide uncluttered main street and behind further fascination lies in the 'castle', a massive earthwork, impressive not only for its size, but for the preserved detail of the defences that surround it. Further round, there are glimpses of the fine hall at Newbold Revel from which an easy track leads on to Easenhall, where uniform, but appealing, estate cottages line the street. Although relatively short, the route passes many secluded corners and is equally suitable for either a half or full day excursion.

Maps: Pathfinders: 936 & 956 or Landranger: 140

Start: Brinklow (SP 437 795)

Distance: 6 miles

Transport: Brinklow and Easenhall receive an infrequent service from Rugby.

Refreshment: There are pubs at Easenhall and Brinklow, where there is also a fish and chip shop. In summer, a tea room opens beside the canal at Hungerfield.

Brinklow straddles the Foss Way, a Roman road that cuts across the heart of England for some 200 miles from Axminster to Lincoln. Although at one time thought to represent a defensible front line for the advancing legions, it is now seen as a route to facilitate cross-country communication and may additionally have served as an extended base line to produce a cartographic survey of the country. The fact that there are no forts or turrets along its length and the argument that such a long frontier would have in any case been impractical to hold, lend weight to the modern theory. It generally follows the line of an ancient trackway and was built in separate sections rather than a single road in about 47 AD by Aulus Plautius, who had led Claudius' conquest of the island in 43

AD. After the Romans had finally quelled Boudicca's rebellion in 60 AD, much of the Midlands settled peacefully to the Roman way of life with villas, farms and towns bringing a new order to the landscape.

From the high street in the centre of Brinklow, leave along a signed path beside the Raven Inn. Over a stile at its end, climb an embankment to enter the outer enclosure of the 'castle'. A trod across open grass leads to a second compound and thence to the central mound.

The hill possibly originated as an ancient burial mound, the name perhaps meaning 'burial mound of Brynca'. The fact that the Fosse Way diverts around it suggests its presence when the Romans arrived. The motte and bailey on its summit, known locally as the Trump, was built by the Mowbray family in about 1135 and is arguably the best surviving example of its type in the country. Any buildings must have been constructed of wood as no evidence of masonry has been found on the site and, unfortunately, no documented account of the castle's history has been found. Rising high above the village, the mound covers an extensive area. On top, an outer

Inner ramparts of 'The Trump'

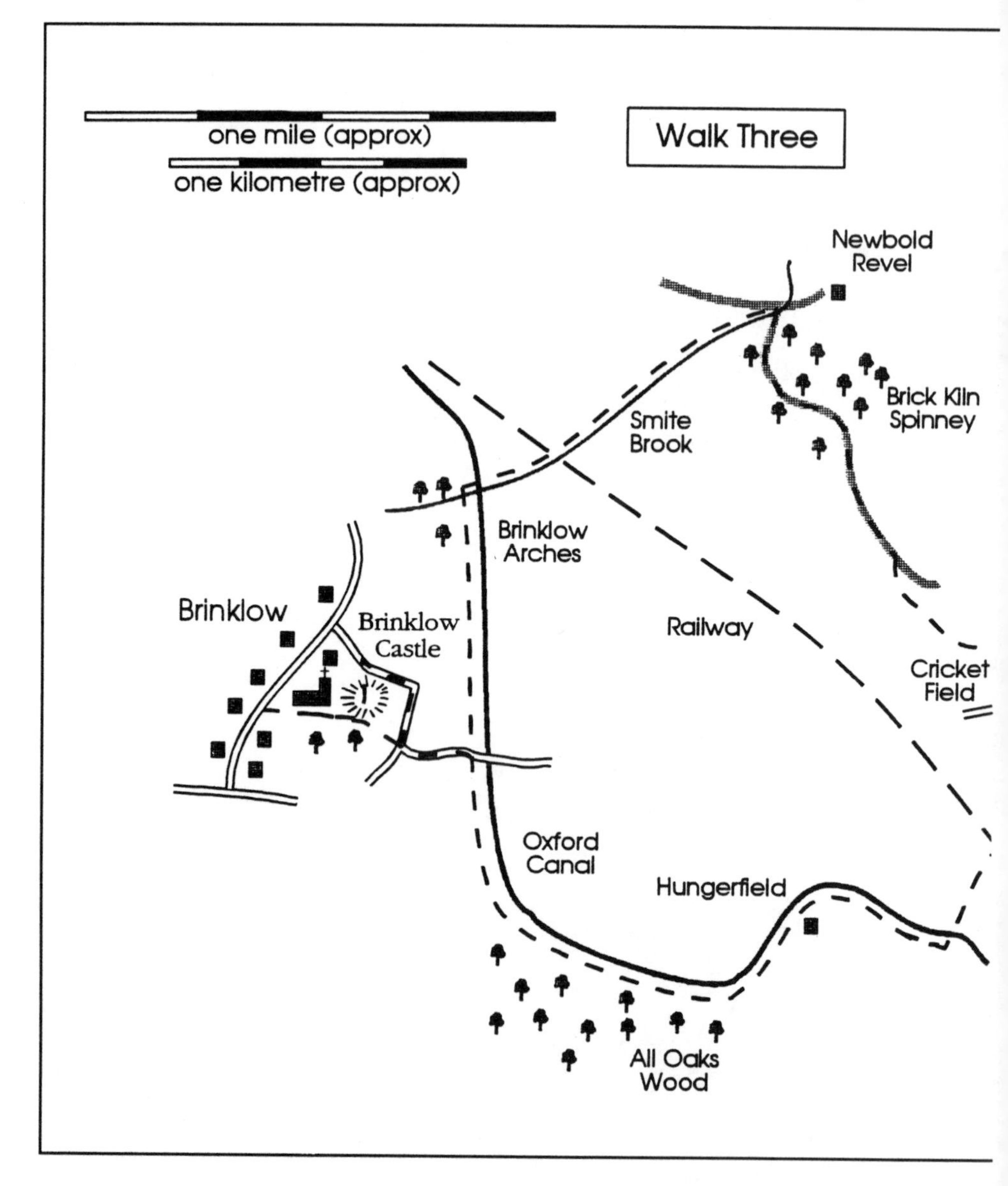

ditch and bank enclose a compound behind which, further defences define a second higher area. A final deep ditch surrounds the central mound, which falls away steeply to the north. From the top

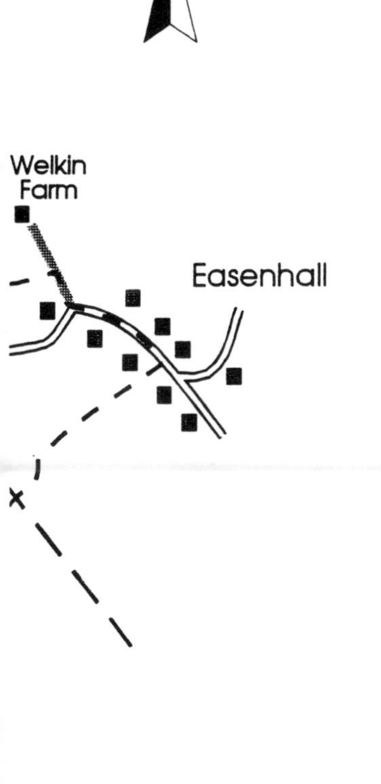

there are extensive views in all directions, the Fosse Way describing a clear line to the south.

The summit was once crowned with elms, but these have sadly gone, a victim of Dutch elm disease, caused by a fungus and spread by the elm bark beetle. In spring, the female beetle, which feeds on elm bark, deposits her eggs below the surface and can carry infecting spores from tree to tree. The feeding grubs produce distinctive feather-like patterns by burrowing between the bark and the wood, but this is harmless and it is the fungus that kills the tree by blocking its internal capillaries and depriving it of nutrients. There is no effective remedy and control methods concentrate on eliminating the beetle. An earlier attack in 1927 was far less damaging, but examination of pollen deposits trapped in the sediments of lakes or peat shows a devastation of the country's elms in about 3000 BC that might have been due to the disease.

Descend its north-western flank to a gate beside Ell lane. Turn right, following it round a bend to a junction and go left, shortly to arrive at a canal bridge. Drop to the canal's towpath and follow it left into a cutting through the eastern end of Brinklow Hill.

When first built, the canal meandered around the village, as suggested by some old street names. To speed traffic during the early nineteenth century, it was shortened along its present line by making this deep cut through Brinklow Hill. Part of the original line of the canal from the village is still visible on the left of the canal beyond the cutting.

Some 300 metres after the cutting, leave the towpath and climb down the embankment on a non-to-obvious path to Smite Brook. Pass underneath the aqueduct and cross a plank bridge to enter a field. Follow the brook beneath a railway bridge and then keep going beside the stream over the next two fields, finally emerging through a gate onto a drive beside Newbold Revel.

From Saxon times, the manor was known as Fenny Newbold and remained so until the last quarter of the twelfth century, when the daughter of Thomas de Wappenbury, its owner, married Robert Revel of Swinford in Leicestershire. Thereafter known as Newbold Revel, it remained with the Revels until it passed in marriage to Sir Stephen Malory in about 1383. His great grandson, Sir Thomas Malory, is credited with the authorship of Morte d'Arthur, one of the masterpieces of English prose and which has inspired many later writers. Only two copies of Caxton's original folio and an independent manuscript are now known to exist. Until his death in 1470, Sir Thomas was a colourful character and, after returning from fighting alongside the Earl of Warwick in the French wars, was imprisoned for quarrels with his neighbours and his anti-Yorkist attitudes. During the sixteenth and early seventeenth centuries, the manor was held by a succession of owners before passing to the Skipwith family. They demolished the old manor house in 1716 and erected the delightfully palatial brick Queen Anne house we see today, in which the family lived until 1862. Following another succession of owners, the estate was broken up and the house became a missionary training centre. The second World War saw it requisitioned for the Royal Air Force and, after demobilisation, it was developed as a teacher training college. The Prison Service acquired it in 1985 and have since restored and developed the mansion and its gardens as a training and conference centre.

The house and grounds are not open to the public, but its imposing facade can be seen through the trees across playing fields and a lake. Housed in the former stable block, the Prison Service has brought together an exhibition depicting the history of imprisonment and punishment since medieval times. Please note that admission is only by prior appointment with the Curator (telephone 01788 834168).

Turn right towards the hall and then immediately go right again through a field gate onto a bridleway. It shortly joins a track from the hall and bends around the periphery of its grounds before passing through Brick Kiln Spinney.

The significance of the name probably indicates that the bricks for the hall were made here. At that time, bricks for the majority of building projects were produced on site, clay and ash being obtained locally and a temporary kiln built for firing. The concept of a large brickworks satisfying a wide market only developed with the canal age, which for the first time, allowed the economic bulk transport of heavy commodities in inland areas.

Beyond, a broad track traverses open fields but is eventually barred by a gate. The footpath follows the fenceline around to the right, finally ending through a gate onto a track. To the right is Easenhall cricket field, walk around this on its left boundary, leaving through a gap to the left of the lodge gate. Turn right and, on meeting the lane, follow it left into the village.

One cannot fail to be impressed by the striking lodge overlooking the cricket green. A copper-capped turret bearing a circular lookout rises beside a tall gable, whose barge-boards are intricately decorated. Elsewhere in the village, the same lavish Victorian architecture is displayed in Gothic windows, polychromatic brick and decorated barge boards. Once part of the Newbold Revel estate, it is a good example of the better kind of living conditions that some estate owners provided for their workers. In contrasting style is the Golden Lion, which dates from 1640 and retains some original wattle and daub walling, and the simple, tiny, non-conformist brick chapel built in 1872 on the opposite side of the road.

Just after the Golden Lion look for a marked footpath through a gap on the right. Pass between houses into the fields and head towards a stark girder footbridge over the railway, some 1/3 mile away. Keep going on a clear track across farmland on the other side to a bridge over the canal and join the towpath going right. It winds first by Hungerfield Bridge and then some

cottages to Cathiron Lane. Beyond, the waterway carries on along the edge of All Oaks Wood, eventually passing through more open countryside to bridge 34, where you first joined the canal. Return to the road and walk back to the junction, but now go ahead over a stile into a ridged meadow. Walk across to another stile in its far right corner. Over that, keep going, now following the curving outer ditch of Brinklow Castle. Climb over a stile at the corner of the field and return to the village by your outward route along a footpath over the stile on your left.

Prior to the Union Chargeability Act of 1865, which broadened responsibility for the poor beyond the immediate parish, Brinklow was known as an 'open village'. Before that Act, each village was required to support its own poor, the burden falling mainly on principle landowners. Where land was concentrated in a single ownership, the lord of the manor was able to minimise his obligation by keeping the population of the village as low as possible commensurate with the need to work his land. As leases expired, cottages were pulled down and settlement only allowed when it was supported by a land holding or long-term work contract. Some landowners resorted to eviction and unsettled labourers and their families were forced to live where they could, often forced to pay high rents for the poor housing that frequently characterised open villages. This left many having to walk considerable distances to their daily work, often to those very villages where they were not permitted to live, in this case, Coombe Fields some two miles away.

Consequently, Brinklow has always been a busy place and was granted a market in 1218 that survived for some 600 years. To satisfy the many residents and visitors, pubs and inns readily sprang up, although their propriety was sometimes questioned. A record of 1646 notes that the seven ale houses were accused of being detrimental to the 'children and servants' of the village, causing them to be 'drawn into many inconveniences and so neglect their callings', and it was ordered that six should be closed. Behaviour must have since improved or else memories grown dim as the number has crept up again. The Oxford Canal at one time passed through the town and brought with it trade and industries such as boat building and candle making. Later, Brinklow provided homes for the miners of Binley Colliery and today is a dormitory for workers in Rugby and Coventry. It remains an attractive village, with many buildings older than they look, their timber-framing concealed by stucco. This practice became fashionable during the latter part of the eighteenth century, giving buildings the appearance of being built of stone.

St John the Baptist's Church literally climbs the western slope of the mound, its floor rising by twelve feet from end to end. It was built in the thirteenth century by Austin Canons from Kenilworth Abbey, an order that involved themselves considerably in pastoral work. Their simple rule is attributed to St Augustine of Hippo, a North African bishop who died in 430. The community experienced a revival in the twelfth century as a reaction to growing dissatisfaction with the Benedictine rule. The church was substantially rebuilt in the fifteenth century and internally altered in the 1860s. Entrance is by the northern sixteenth-century wooden porch, whose outer doors were designed to discourage sheep who might otherwise be inclined to join the service. The arms above the ancient oak door are those of George IV. In the south aisle, notice heart-shaped faces that gaze down from the roof, and on either side of the chancel arch are an unusual pair of Victorian stone ambos or pulpits. Behind the southern one rises a fine rood staircase. These were common in medieval churches, giving access to a gallery across the entrance to the choir which carried a great crucifix symbolising Christ's victory. It also separated the congregation, who in those days were mere onlookers, from the ceremony and ritual carried out by the priests at the altar. Most of these screens were pulled down at the reformation and few originals survive in this country. In the chancel, beneath the carpet are wooden traps covering two tombs and the walls by the altar are decorated with pretty Victorian Minton tiles.

Walk 4: Kingswood, Lapworth, Packwood, Baddesley Clinton, Wroxall and Rowington

Once deep within the Forest of Arden, the early settlements hereabouts were centred on small woodland clearings, often used for summer pasture rather than cultivation. Gradual deforestation has opened up a gently rolling topography, the landscape remaining pleasantly broken by hedgerow trees and smaller copses which make attractive habitats for a diverse range of animals, birds and plants. Despite its proximity to the Birmingham conurbation, the area has as yet escaped large-scale dormitory development and retains its rural atmosphere.

This walk explores some of its diversity, passing a church and house that each well-justify claims to being the finest in the county. Remnants of ancient forest contrast with the canals of the industrial revolution and are complemented by examples of Victorian architecture at both ends of the social spectrum.

Canal towpaths as well as field paths and tracks feature in this walk and the short inevitable stretches along lanes are not arduous. Although long in its entirety, its figure-of-eight pattern ideally allows the walk to be considered as two separate expeditions, thus allowing more time if you wish to visit the National Trust houses at Packwood and Baddesley Clinton. A note is given at the appropriate point in the text.

Maps: Pathfinders: 954, 955, 975 & 976 or Landranger: 139

Start: Car-park at Kingswood Junction (Map Reference SP 186 709)

Distance: 12½ miles or two walks of 6½ and 7 miles

Transport: Local bus services from Leamington are infrequent, but the station at Lapworth is served from Birmingham and Leamington.

Refreshment: Inns lie beside the Stratford Canal at Lapworth and the Grand Union Canal near Kingswood and Turner's Green. Light meals and refreshments are also available at Baddesley Clinton during the summer months when the house is open.

The Stratford Canal, constructed between 1796 and 1816, arrived at Kingswood in 1802 and carried cargoes of coal, bricks and salt as well as supplies for Cadbury's chocolate factory at Bournville. It here passed close to the Warwick and Birmingham Canal (now part of the Grand Union) and a short link between the two brought the importance of a junction to Kingswood. As unfettered co-operation between canal companies was a rare thing, the connecting cut was made through a lock behind the northern of the two cottages on the eastern bank. Through this, the Warwick Canal gained with some 25,000 gallons of water each time a boat passed between the two, a sizeable 'payment' as water shortages were often a problem. Recent refurbishment work has re-opened a lower stop lock abandoned in 1818 and restored the canal-side workshops and toll offices. At one time, a number of people were employed in the maintenance yards or on collecting tolls from passing traffic. A story tells that one afternoon, the foreman being in a holiday mood, went with his workers into one of the pubs in town. Unfortunately, one of the managers appeared and, taking a less generous view of the matter, dismissed him on the spot.

Although built 'on the cheap', the Stratford Canal cost far more than anticipated and never realised its expected return. By 1825, its original £75 shares had fallen in value to £16 10s and in 1856, the company sold out to the Oxford, Worcester and Wolverhampton Railway Company, later incorporated within the Great Western Railway. The closure in 1873 of the Avon Navigation, linking the canal to the River Severn and thus the sea trading port of Bristol, struck another blow and the last commercial cargo was unloaded here on Christmas Eve in 1929. In the face of a decision to close what remained of the waterway in 1958, a restoration scheme using volunteer labour was put forward. When the National Trust re-opened the canal in 1964, the renovation work had cost just half that estimated for the complete closure. More lately, the Avon Navigation has also been re-opened and the waterway is once again busy with the passage of thousands of boats each year.

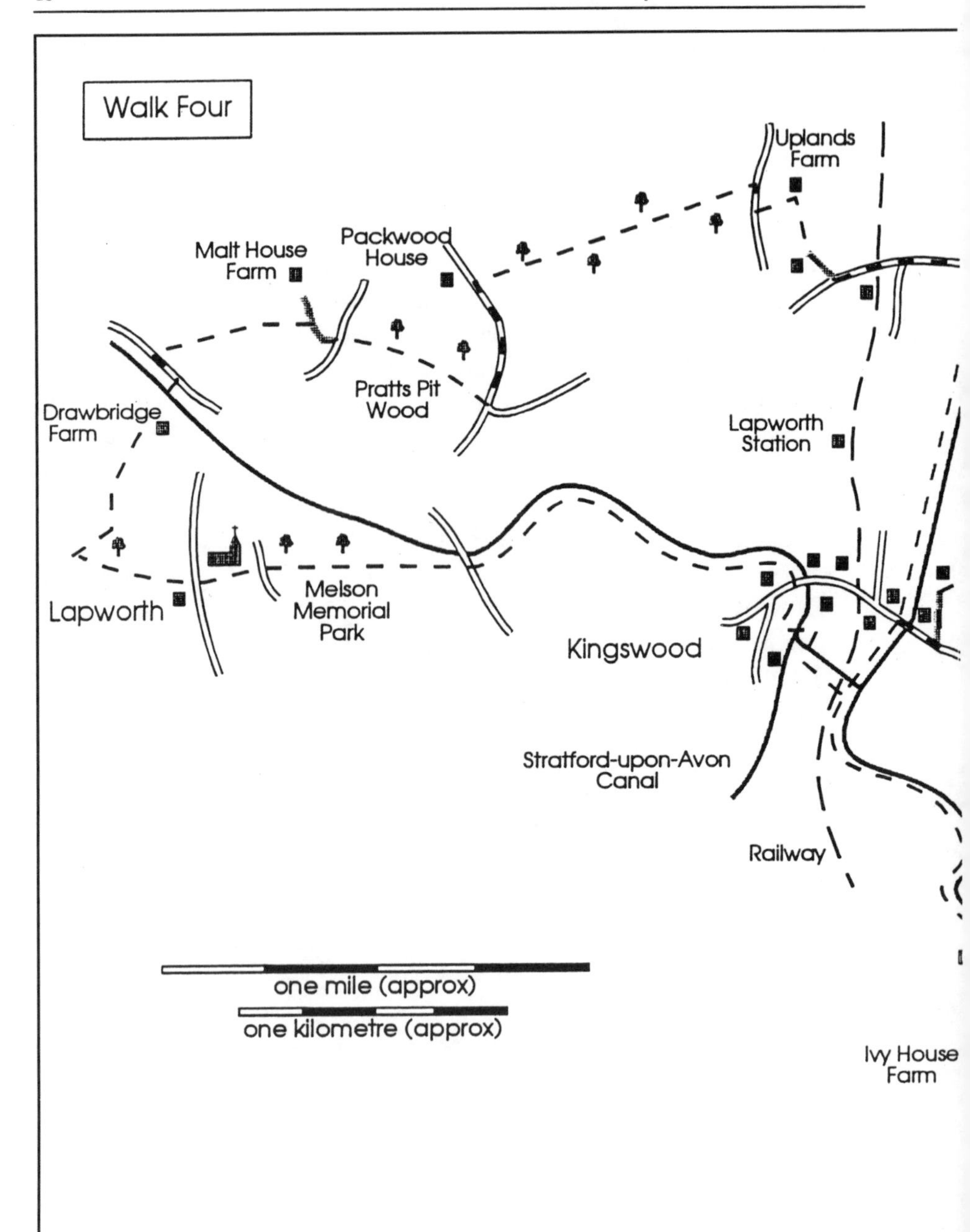

Walk Four
Uplands Farm
Packwood House
Malt House Farm
Pratts Pit Wood
Drawbridge Farm
Lapworth Station
Lapworth
Melson Memorial Park
Kingswood
Stratford-upon-Avon Canal
Railway
one mile (approx)
one kilometre (approx)
Ivy House Farm

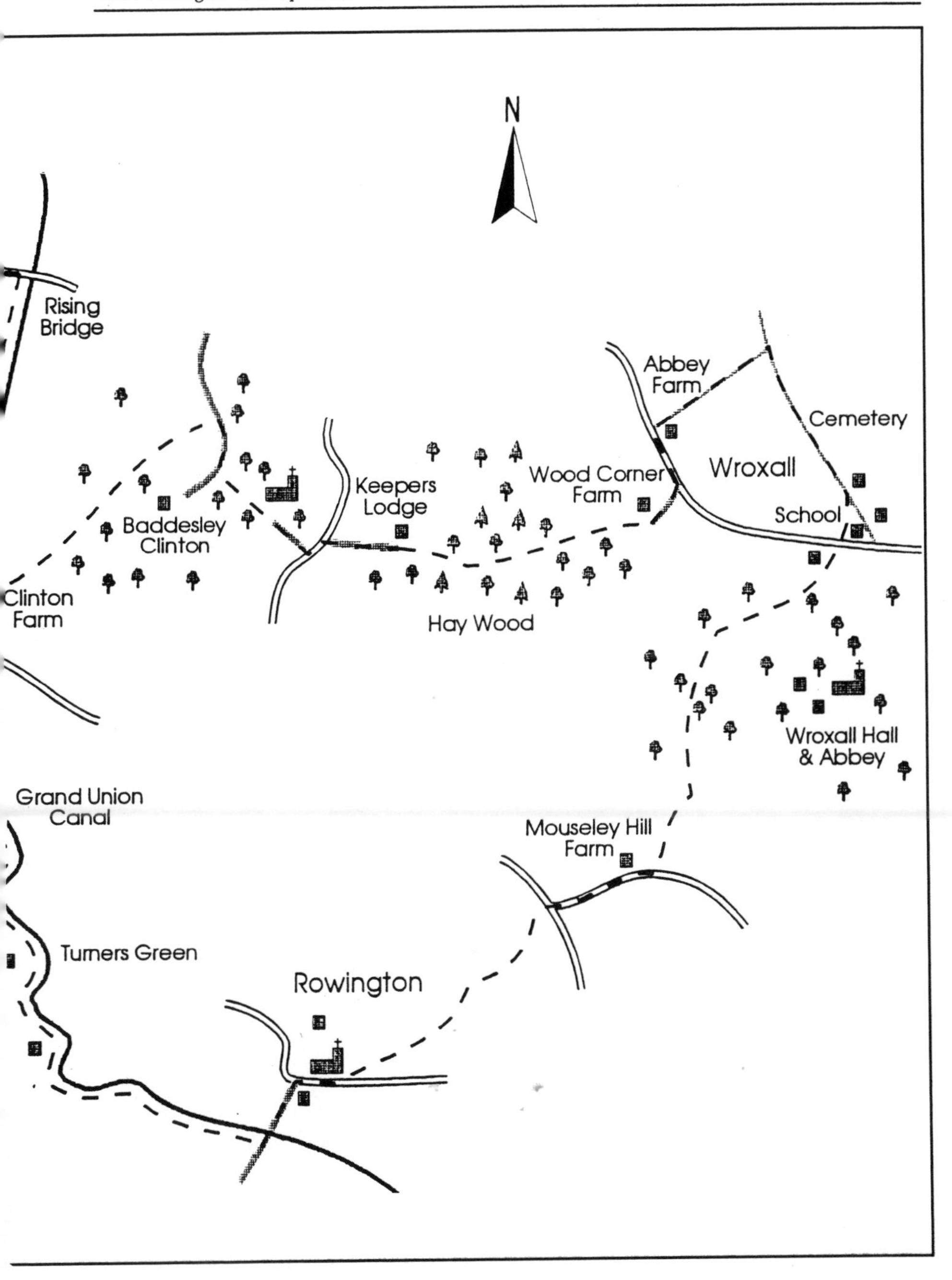
N
Rising Bridge
Abbey Farm
Cemetery
Wroxall
Wood Corner Farm
Keepers Lodge
School
Baddesley Clinton
Clinton Farm
Hay Wood
Wroxall Hall & Abbey
Grand Union Canal
Mouseley Hill Farm
Turners Green
Rowington

The Birmingham to Oxford Junction railway reached Kingswood in 1852, adding railway workers to the inhabitants of what had become a canal village. By the beginning of the twentieth century, wealthy Birmingham business-men were also building villas here, preferring to commute rather than live in their increasingly industrialised city. The increasing busyness of the station led to it being renamed Lapworth in 1913, allegedly to distinguish it from Kingswood in Gloucestershire, and the village has now become synonymous with Lapworth.

Yet, Kingswood's history is far older than the industrial revolution. In the fields to the east of the canal are some scanty remains of Harborough Banks, a large earthwork. Known to be the site of both British and Roman camps it is also said to be on a ley, an alignment of ancient sacred sites. Neolithic and Iron Age relics have been found there, including a ewer, axe head and in 1824, a hoard of Celtic coins.

From the car park beside the basin join the towpath and turn left. The canal passes underneath the road before rising through a succession of locks. At lock 14, an iron split bridge takes the towpath onto the opposite bank near The Boot Inn. Beyond, more locks again raise the canal some 35 metres above Kingswood, after which it runs level for a short distance to re-pass under the main road at bridge number 31.

Notice, as you climb beside the locks, that many have an adjacent basin. Its purpose was twofold, firstly as a reservoir to store the water necessary to supply closely grouped locks and secondly to allow barges to pass each other, since it is considerably more efficient to alternate up and down traffic through each lock.

Leave the canal up a track immediately after the bridge, crossing into a paddock on the right just before the road. Follow the left-hand hedge to its bottom corner and keep going across the next field to Lapworth cricket green.

Called the Melson Memorial Park in memory of Alfred Duckworth Melson, who bequeathed it in 1928 for the enjoyment of the people of Lapworth. He stipulated that it could be used for any sport except football, as he noted that spectators of that game were wont to drop cigarette packets. His generosity also provided land for the nearby War Memorial.

Leave by a stile in the far left corner, walking ahead past two oaks and then following a hedge to another stile. Beyond, a grass trod roughly parallels the field's left boundary, dropping to leave beyond a tree-fringed pond. The way is then waymarked beside a second pond and across the bottom of a house lawn to a high hedge. Through that, climb to the top right corner of the meadow to emerge at a lane. A hand-gate to the right of the drive opposite leads to Lapworth's church.

In the Domesday Book, Lapworth appears as Lapeforde and was then still mainly woodland. Clearances for small fields and enclosures followed, but the poor quality of the land left much of it fit only for pasture, a characteristic that remains today.

The Church of St Mary the Virgin is reputedly the finest in Warwickshire. A lovely compact building in a delightful setting, its spire playing hide and seek amongst the trees as you approach from afar. From a small nave and chancel in the 1100s, successive builders have added chapels, aisles and a tower, as well as elevating the roof. The west porch, added in the thirteenth century, is also interesting. It has a small reliquary chapel above and visiting pilgrims processed through by climbing and descending the separate spiral staircases set in the outer wall. The embattled north tower and spire were raised in the fifteenth century and it was only during the last century that it was connected to the main body of the church. A fragment of a Norman window arch, part of the original building, can be seen above a pillar supporting the northern clerestory. As you wander around, stop to admire the alabaster reredos showing the Last Supper and look up to tiny faces, peering down over shields.

Lapworth has a strong association with the Gunpowder Plot as its conceiver, Robert Catesby, was born in 1573 at Bushwood Hall, about 1½ miles south-east of the church. With the ascension of James I, the Catholics had hoped for a relaxation of the increasingly harsh recusancy laws and persecution that they had suffered under Elizabeth. However, on the advice of his ministers, James applied them with even more vigour and a fruitless appeal to Spain was made by Guy Fawkes and others for intervention. In 1604, Catesby devised a plan to assassinate the king and government and install a Catholic regent to the throne. He began to gather support and, by the end of that year, had started digging a tunnel under the parliament building from a rented adjacent house. The work proved to be too much and the plan was in danger of collapsing in 1605 when Thomas Percy, one of the supporters, managed to hire a cellar actually underneath parliament. Two and a half tons of gunpowder were brought in in readiness for an explosion on 5th November, the opening of Parliament, and an uprising in the Midlands was planned to coincide with the resulting confusion. However, the plot was discovered. Tradition attributes it to a warning letter sent by one of the conspirators to Mounteagle, a Catholic peer. Other theories point to spies of Lord Cecil, the Secretary of State, infiltrating the group, or even inciting the plot in the first place to foster further hostility against Catholics. Whatever, Fawkes was arrested as he made his final preparations and the leading conspirators were pursued across the Midlands as they attempted to escape into Wales. Four of them, including Catesby, were killed and the remainder arrested, to be executed with Fawkes in 1606. Fanned by the outrage, religious persecution and discrimination continued well into the following century. Catesby's bones lie in a table tomb by the church door.

From the road, opposite the church to the right of the rectory, a stile leads to a meadow. Walk to a gate at its bottom and then keep going over the hill in the next field to a stile at its far side. Through that, turn right and climb beside a ditch up this and the next field. Then, over another stile, cross diagonally to the far corner behind the high point of the field and, ignoring the gate on the right, go through one ahead to follow a hedge towards

Drawbridge Farm. Leaving the fields, a track through the farm crosses the canal by the 'drawbridge', a modern replacement, to the road. Turn left, going only a short distance before leaving by a way-marked stile on the right into a meadow. Walk ahead, keeping to the left as it broadens. Through a gap, go to a stile in the top right corner of the next field and then follow the hedge on the left, leaving through an opening onto a drive by Malt House Farm. Turn right and walk to the lane at its end. Cross the stile directly opposite into parkland behind Packwood House and walk ahead, shortly joining and then following the right-hand fence line to a ranch stile.

Packwood House lies to the left at the head of its ornamental lake. There is no permitted access to the grounds from here, although if you visit the house, you can then wander around the grounds and gardens.

Cross into a field and follow its left boundary, eventually reaching another stile. Cross that, a stream and a second stile into a meadow and walk up toward the house ahead, keeping to the left side. The path passes left of the house, following the edge of its garden to a final stile and a lane. Turn left and walk to Packwood house, about a third of a mile away.

Before Henry's Dissolution of the monasteries in the 1530s, Packwood estate was owned by the Benedictine priory at Coventry. It then passed through the Sheldons of Beoley to the Fetherston family who, towards the end of the sixteenth century, constructed the timber-framed Tudor manor. Its famous yew garden, said to depict the Sermon on the Mount, was originally laid out in about 1650 by John Fetherston, although only the raised southern part, representing the Apostles, Evangelists and Christ, can be attributed to him with any certainty. The yews in the lower part, identified with the multitude, are believed to have been planted in the last century to replace an old orchard and the biblical allusion has possibly only developed since that time. In 1905, Alfred Ash, a Birmingham industrialist, bought the house for his son Graham Baron. He wanted to restore its former Tudor splendour and effectively re-used materials from other period buildings to give authenticity. He also acquired furniture, much of it from Baddesley Clinton, whose contents were being sold to support the maintenance of its estate. After the war, he gave the property and contents for preservation to the National Trust.

Inevitably, traditions have grown around the hospitality given to the passing rich and famous. Queen Elizabeth is improbably reputed to have slept here on her way to visit Robert Dudley, Earl of Leicester, at Kenilworth Castle. Entertaining her and her entourage cost Dudley £1,000 a day and many of the nobility must have regarded the prospect of a royal visit as only marginally preferable to a kiss of death. It is certain, however, that Ireton, one of Essex's generals slept here before the battle at Edge Hill. This put John Fetherston in somewhat of a quandary, since he was undecided on which side to hang his colours. In order to avoid having to provide arms and armour for the Roundheads, he put his armoury in the care of a neighbour. It is said that he eased his conscience by providing hospitality to the defeated Charles II after the Battle of Worcester nine years later.

It is a delight to walk past here in early spring, when the lawns on either side of the road are ablaze with yellow daffodils. They have been planted as part of the Fields of Hope campaign to raise money for the nearby Warren Pearl Hospice and other cancer charities.

Directly opposite the entrance to the house, across the grass on the right, brick steps rise to a wrought iron gate from which a tree-lined avenue crosses the park. Part way along, two stiles enclose a short causeway across a pond and, at the end, a stile leads to a lane.

From the house, the avenue is of fine mature oak, but beyond the pond, the trees are younger and include lime. These impart a wonderful scent in summer as the wind excites delicate flowers, hiding amongst the leaves. The scent is particularly attractive to bees, whose persistent drone adds to the sleepiness of a hot afternoon.

Turn right and then immediately go left along a drive to Upland's Farm. Before reaching the buildings, follow a way-mark to the right, shortly crossing a gravel drive. Keep ahead, now on a grass path around the edge of

Packwood's daffodils

the field, eventually leaving through a kissing-gate onto a drive. Go through another kissing-gate diagonally opposite, beyond which a grass path follows the outside perimeter of a garden to a second drive. Walk from the house to a road and turn left, following it to Rising Bridge over the Grand Union Canal, about a third of a mile away. Immediately before the bridge, drop through a gate on the right to the tow path and turn right. A long, straight stretch of canal runs to the next bridge, immediately after which, climb up to the road.

Although making no specific claim to be the 'Heart of England', Kingswood does, in fact, lie on its watershed. A careful study of the map shows that a brook beside the canal flows in both directions. To the north, by way of Cuttle Brook, the rivers Blythe, Trent and Humber, it finally issues into the North Sea at Hull. It also flows south, eventually joining the Alne. Via the succession of the Arrow, Trent and Severn, it then ultimately finds its way into the Bristol Channel.

If you wish to return to Kingswood, remain with the canal as far as the link canal and then turn right to go back to Kingswood Basin.

Walk right past the Navigation Inn and then just beyond the speed restriction sign, turn left on way-marked track to a stable yard. To the right of the stables, a stile leads to a rising paddock. Walk diagonally up to another stile at its top corner. Beyond, keep going alongside the top boundary, shortly crossing a culverted brook enclosed between a pair of stiles. Further on, after crossing another stile, the way reaches a shallow ditch, where the boundary, now enclosing the grounds of Baddesley Clinton, turns away to the right. However, maintain your direction, striking across the meadow to a stile in the far fence. Cross onto a drive and turn right towards Baddesley Clinton, keeping left when it splits to go past the car park entrance.

You should tarry a while so as not to miss the beauty of this splendid medieval moated manor house, much of it dating from the fifteenth and sixteenth centuries. Elegant Tudor brick chimneys rise above grey stone and oak timber-frame walls, from which mullioned windows gaze to their shimmering reflections in the water below. Although the battlements adorning the tower above its entrance may be a nineteenth-century embellishment and all trace of its drawbridge gone, loopholes on either side serve to remind that the house was once as much defensive as domestic. Inside, wooden panelling, carvings and furnishings speak of comfortable refinement and a central courtyard garden, enclosed by the house on three sides is a perfect delight. It is planted in the heraldic colours of the Ferrers family, who held the manor for fifteen generations before it passed to the National Trust. Many Catholic houses have a priest hole, but this has three as well as a secret staircase. Nicholas Owen, a master in the design of such hiding places, converted a passage below the west wing that had previously been a sewer for the garderobes. It served to conceal visiting priests from the pursuivants on more than one occasion, but Owen himself was less fortunate. He was one of those caught in the searches following the Gunpowder Plot and died under torture in the Tower of London, refusing to reveal the locations of his priest holes.

A signed footpath on the left leads to the nearby church.

It is believed a church stood here in Saxon times, although the present building has its origins in the thirteenth century. Major alterations were undertaken at the end of the fifteenth century, when Nicholas Brome, whose family held the manor prior to the Ferrers, added the tower, elevated the nave and inserted clerestory windows. His munificence was in expiation of his guilt for killing a priest, whom he discovered 'in his plor chockinge his wife under ye chinne'. He requested that he be interred upright beneath the doorway, so that 'people may tread upon mee when they come into the Church'. It amused the present incumbent to be told 'mind how you go with her Ladyship' when he assumed his appointment. The chancel was remodelled and the rood screen installed by Edward Ferrers in 1634, the money for the work possibly coming from his marriage union with the Peytos. The beautiful east window shows the families of Nicholas Brome and Sir Edward Ferrers, whose marriage to Constance, Brome's daughter, began the long association of the Ferrers with Baddesley. A tablet, recording Edward Ferrers' rebuilding work, notes that the church was first consecrated for St James. The dedication was changed to St Michael 1872 when the building was restored after some years of neglect.

Leave the churchyard through a kissing-gate on the far side and walk to the road.

Originally, the village is thought to have been near the church and was possibly moved, as were many settlements, to create greater privacy around the manor house. The pasture to the south-west shows traces of ancient strip agriculture and the drive from the church is known locally as a 'fordrough', an old word describing a short wide lane leading to fields. Lining the drive are some sweet chestnut trees, from which in summer, dangle delicate catkins. Although its autumn fruit appears similar to that of the horse chestnut or conker tree, the two are not related. Their leaves and flowers are very different, but more importantly, chestnuts make extremely good eating, no doubt a factor appreciated by the Romans who first brought the tree to these shores.

Go left, but after a few metres, turn right onto a farm track leading to Keeper's Lodge and Hay Wood, carrying on beyond into the trees. Ignore a broad crossing track in the middle and keep going to the far edge of the wood, leaving through a gate.

Hay Wood is one of the last vestiges of Shakespeare's Arden Forest, a sylvan carpet that once covered some two hundred square miles between the Avon and Tame rivers. From Roman times, small settlement clearings were made deep in the woods and many of the moated enclosures that now dot the surrounding country-side identify later Norman settlements. In fact, the name Bad-desley derives from 'woodland clearing of Bæddi'. Since medieval times, much of the deforestation was caused by the production of charcoal to fuel the early Midlands iron industry. By the end of the eighteenth century, the forests had gone and the general pattern was little different from that seen today, small copses and hedge-row trees surviving as remnants of that ancient woodland. Once part of the Baddesley estate, it is now managed by Forest Enter-prise and, although its composition bears little relation to the original 'wild wood' there is a surprising variety in the vegetation, both great and small.

Now in a field, walk to a gate on the far side, just to the right of Wood Corner Farm. Carry on beside the buildings and go through a second gate onto a track. Turn left and follow it past the farm, bending right to finally emerge on a road. Abbey Farm lies a short distance to the left. Go through its second entrance, where waymarks identify the path past the barns and along a field track behind. At its end, turn right to the tiny hamlet of Wroxall.

In 1861, James Dugdale, from Dovecote just outside Liverpool, bought Wroxall Abbey, and in contrast to the grand mansion he built for himself, created this delightful collection of estate cot-tages, a school and other buildings in polychromatic brick. The mid-nineteenth century saw a revival in the use of exposed brick, which during the preceding Regency period had often disappeared behind stucco. Encouraged by improved production techniques, cheap canal and railway distribution and the repeal of the Brick Tax in 1850, architectural fashion once again began to explore the versatility of brick. Dugdale's assortment of buildings combine utility with an absorbing interplay of colour and shape that is often lacking in modern vernacular.

Shortly before the track ends, look for a stile on the right. A path crosses the field behind the school, emerging on the main road. Opposite, a track signed to Quarry Lane goes over a stile into Wroxall Abbey Park, keep going to eventually arrive at a gate.

Wroxall church and hall lie to the left across the park. A Benedictine Nunnery was founded here in 1141 by Hugh Fitz Richard of nearby Hatton in gratitude for his release after seven years imprisonment in the Holy Land. Legend says that, after praying to St Leonard, the patron of prisoners, for deliverance, the Saint appeared and a bargain was struck, freedom in exchange for him establishing a religious house. Still in chains, he was miraculously brought home and in a vision, shown the site where he was to build. Today, little remains of that abbey. The simple stone church, with its embattled part-brick tower, is a remnant of the great abbey church's north aisle. On the other side of the path, concealed in the vegetation, are fragments of the cloisters and chapter house. Inside, an array of memorials to the Dugdale and Wren families look down from the walls which rise to a wooden tie-beamed roof. A Victorian screen divides the church and beyond it are choir stalls embellished with interesting carvings. Behind the alter, a stone reredos shows Christ with four angels and the evangelists and, in the windows, saints and scenes from His life are depicted in medieval glass. Christopher Wren bought the abbey when he was eighty-two, three years after completing St Paul's. He is credited with the gracefully bayed brick wall that encloses the garden on the north side. Wroxall remained with his descendants until Dugdale's ownership. He demolished an old Elizabethan house that had stood by the church and built the imposing brick mansion and stables that now dominate the estate. More lately the house has seen two private schools and is now being developed as a recreation centre.

Go through the gate and head for a small enclosed wood. Once through, bear left to a solitary ash and then fork left again across the park to a kissing gate in the far fence.

From this point there is a fine view across the park to Dugdale's grand house.

Maintaining your line across the meadow, pass a line of mature oaks to a gap in the hedge, go through and turn left, climbing up the hill to cross a double stile. Turn right and follow the hedge, ignoring waymarked paths leaving on either side, and finally emerge onto a lane. Turn right and walk past Mousley Hill Farm and again go right at a junction. A few metres on, leave over a stile on the left and follow the hedge away from the road. The way, shortly joined by a stream, eventually reaches another stile. Follow the stream around the next field, ignoring a bridge on the right, to a second bridge and stile in the far corner. Now head for St Laurence's Church at Rowington, clearly visible on the higher ground, leaving the final field over a stile into the eastern end of its churchyard.

From an early Saxon forest clearing, Rowington has remained a small settlement and from the twelfth century until the Dissolution, a community of Cistercian nuns was settled here. The church standing proud atop Culvers Hill can be traced to those earliest days, although today's building is a mix of later styles and was extensively restored in the 1870s. Unusually, the twelfth-century square embattled tower rises from the eastern end of the nave rather than the west. The chancel is particularly pleasing, illuminated by a beautiful east window depicting saints and having a ceiling decorated with gilt suns and stars. The brick and stucco Victorian vicarage beside the churchyard has an elegant dutch-style east gable, gazing out over a ha-ha-type wall across the valley. As the church is generally closed, it is worth passing this way on a Sunday.

Rowington claims association with William Shakespeare in its half-timbered Shakespeare Hall, lying about two-thirds of a mile to the north of the church. The family name first appeared in the area in 1485 and, during a fifty-five year period around the end of the sixteenth century, four Williams are recorded as having lived there. The family appeared to be related to the play-wright and there is a claim that William wrote 'As You Like It' in the house, believe it or not – as you like.

A bridleway leaves the main road opposite the south-west corner of the churchyard to the Grand Union Canal. Join the towpath on its far bank and follow it west into the cutting.

In 1929, the Grand Union Company was formed which, by amalgamating several existing routes into single ownership, established a continuous line from Wapping to Birmingham. In its original form, wider barges could only be accommodated up to Braunston, being constrained thereafter by the narrow gauge of the Birmingham system. An extensive programme of widening was instituted in the 1930s, but the many locks and bridges within the Birmingham Navigations represented a prohibitive cost and the broad gauge was only taken to the outskirts of the city. Even then, other parts of the waterway were often not wide enough to allow two broad-beam boats to pass. Thus, the efficiency of large boats carrying greater cargo was never realised and most traffic ran as breasted pairs of narrow-boats. The war halted further development and its fate as a commercial waterway was sealed. Yet, it is still busy with pleasure craft, which perpetuate the tradition of sporting striking liveries and brightly coloured scenes established by the working boatmen. The early canals, wherever possible, followed the contours of the land. Although these routes were relatively cheap and minimised construction problems, it meant that journey times were often long. The later engineers were bolder, tackling obstacles head on, as in this cutting that runs for some three-quarters of a mile through Rowington Hill. Its unmanaged steep banks, although enjoying little sun, allow a variety of more natural vegetation to develop.

Beyond the cutting, the canal gently meanders through open countryside following the lie of the land. Eventually the waterway is joined by the railway and widens to a junction. The Grand Union continues north to Birmingham, but to the left, a short channel passes underneath the railway to unite it with the Stratford Canal.

The cast iron sluice control to the left of the path, seemingly serving no purpose, was one of many that allowed isolated sections of the canal to be drained for repair. The run-off channel lies through the undergrowth below the towpath.

Cross the bridge at the far end of the link and walk up by the old lock to the Stratford Canal. The car park lies a short distance to the right on the opposite bank.

Walk 5: Bubbenhall, Wappenbury, Hunningham and Weston under Wetherley

Although only a short distance to the south of Coventry, this quiet corner of Warwickshire has been relatively neglected by the encroaching steal of urbanisation. Even in Bubbenhall, where modern estate houses far outnumber the old cottages, there remain pleasing corners to attract the eye. Across the fields, the other villages included within this round appear forgotten, and long may they remain so. The route passes through two small woods, Wappenbury and Bubbenhall, both of which provide interesting diversions to the general openness of the countryside.

Maps: Pathfinders: 955 & 976 or Landrangers: 140 & 151

Start: Paget's Lane off the A445, south-east of Bubbenhall (Map Reference SP 364 723)

Distance: 8 miles

Transport: Services from Coventry and Leamington are infrequent.

Refreshment: There are pubs at Bubbenhall and Hunningham.

Walk away from the main road along Paget's Lane, branching left where it later forks. At the end of the paved way, go through a gate to the right of the entrance to Shrubs Lodge. Follow an ensuing bridleway that shortly leads through the north-eastern corner of Wappenbury Wood.

The wood is now managed by Forest Enterprise and Warwickshire Wildlife Trust and visitors without dogs are welcome to walk into it other than on Wednesdays and Saturdays. The restrictions do not, of course, apply to Rights of Way and therefore this walk is unaffected. The wood extends over some 400 acres and provides a home to a variety of plants and wildlife. Over 20 species of butterfly have been recorded and some of the less common birds that you might see include the lesser spotted woodpecker, nightingale and woodcock. The woodland is diverse and worthy of exploration.

Emerging through a gate on the far side, walk ahead to join a gravel farm track that continues to a junction. Keep going onwards along a waymarked grass path that delves through more trees, also part of the reserve. At a split, go left, shortly leaving the trees through a gate for a grass field. A trod then guides the way to a clump of trees in the far corner, beyond which a dirt track leads to a lane facing Hill Farm. Go through a field gate directly opposite and walk away from the road, swapping to the other side of the hedge through a gap part-way down. Beyond a gate at the bottom, mount a stile on the right and walk ahead across the next two fields. Leave the third field by the second of two gates passed on the right, and then with the hedge on your left, carry on to emerge on a lane at Wappenbury. Go left to the junction and then turn in front of Wappenbury Hall towards the church of St John the Baptist, down the lane on the right.

Wappenbury Hall

Although not immediately obvious from your approach, Wappenbury is the site of a very ancient settlement, a hillfort. Its builders exploited an area of naturally higher ground, conveniently defended on two sides by water courses. Only on the northern and eastern sides did they need to construct bank and ditch fortifications whilst to the south, they enhanced the already steep banks of the River Leam by the addition of a rampart. The most conspicuous surviving features lie above the river, where the entrance, guarded by inward turning wings, is clearly evident. The path to Hunningham leaves through it. The roughly square 8 hectare site is now occupied by a farm, some cottages and two churches but the original date of settlement is uncertain. Finds of a stone axe, flint arrow head, pottery and the remains of some kilns suggest occupation extending from the Iron Age until the departure of the Romans in about 300 AD or 400 AD. That the site was again inhabited during medieval times is indicated by ridges and furrows in some of the surrounding fields and the discovery of a number of house platforms and hollow ways, one of which continues in use as the lane east of St John's Church. The village was abandoned after 1349, when the Black Death reportedly killed some 250 of the inhabitants. The few survivors moved on, leaving their wattle and daub cottages to crumble away.

Wappenbury's two churches tell something of the history of Catholicism in this part of the Midlands. St John's Church, dating from the thirteenth century, was held by the Benedictine priory at Monks Kirby and was, as indeed were all pre-sixteenth-century churches, part of the Roman church. Henry VIII's Reformation broke that tie, establishing the Church in England. During the following centuries, adherents to the 'old faith' were persecuted. However, Wappenbury's manor passed to a Catholic family, the Morgans, and periodic secret celebrations of the Mass continued in the attic of a small house by the Leam, attracting a discrete congregation from as far afield as Coventry and Rugby. In 1734 a small mission with a resident priest was established from which the surrounding towns were served for the next hundred years. In 1849, St Anne's was built and the early mission was incorporated within the presbytery. It

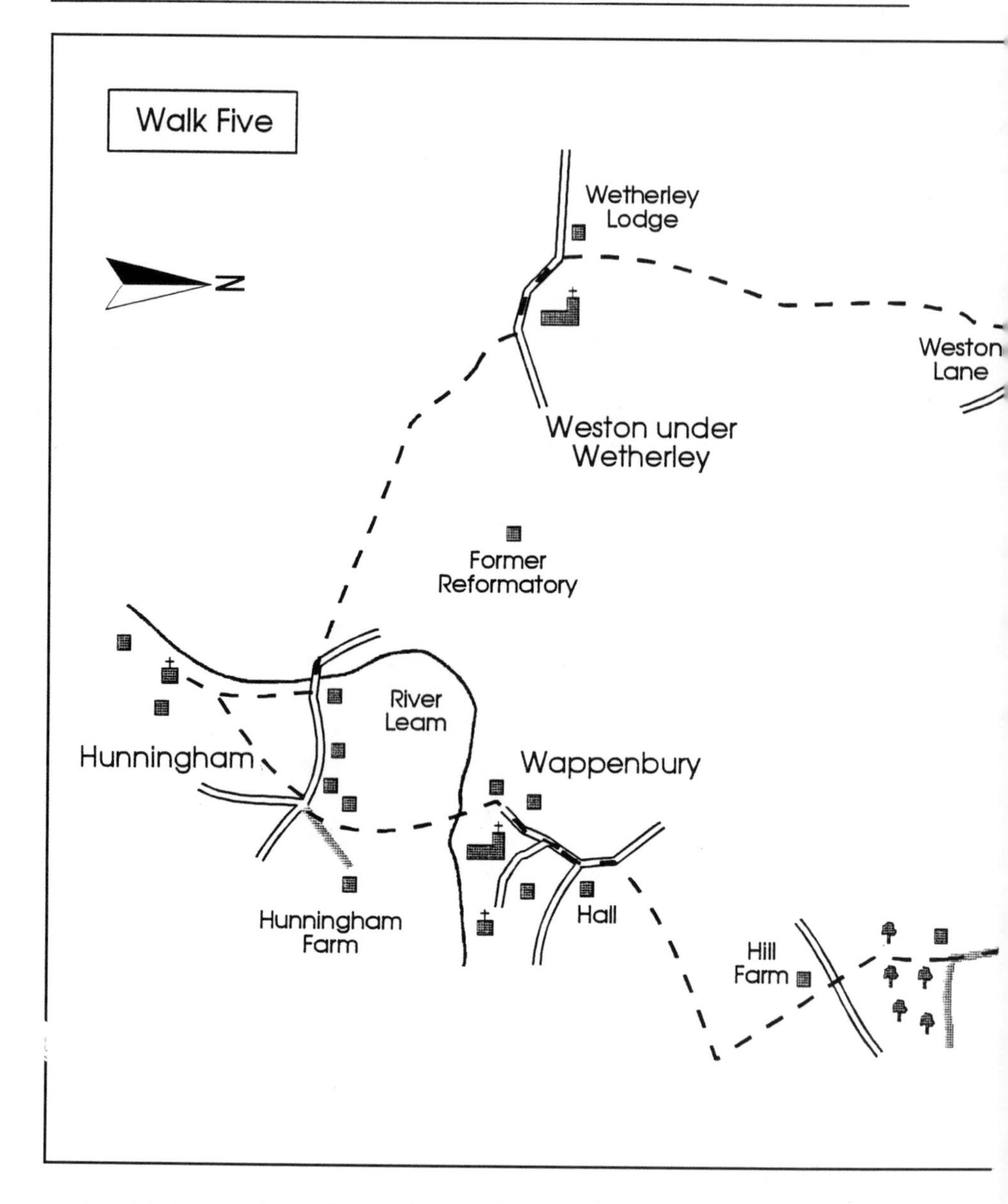

humbly bears the title, the 'jewel of the Catholic Church of Warwickshire', recognising Wappenbury's place in Catholic history.

The oldest parts of St John's lie in the chancel and nave, with the

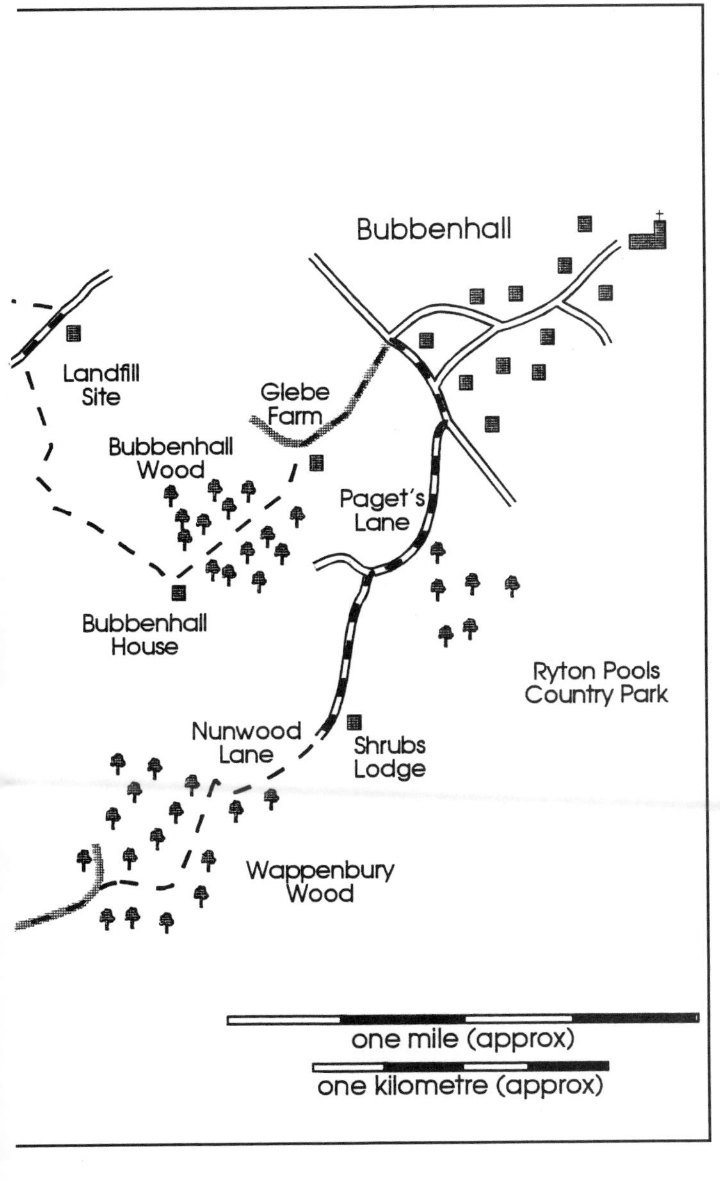

tower and arcade being added in the fourteenth century. The substantial alterations of the nineteenth century, derived their inspiration from the original architectural style and there is thus some apparent harmony. The marble memorials, now below the tower, were removed from the body of the church at that time. One illustrates the high child mortality of the nineteenth century and interestingly records the premature deaths of Edith Oldham and four siblings, who were born in Cairo shortly before the building of the Suez Canal. Two thirteenth-century coffin lids stand against the wall, both are decorated with crosses and the smaller one was obviously for a child. On the high arch below the tower a pig's head looks down and, worked into a capital, is a grotesque face. Outside, more bizarre images decorate the embattled tower and the remains of an old cross stand to the south of the church.

St Anne's, which lies to the east is, by contrast, a simple but elegant brick building attributed to the architect Pugin. Born of French and English parents and a Catholic convert, he developed a 'mechanistic' approach to architecture, equating beauty with structural honesty. His ideas significantly influenced the Gothic Revival and Arts and Crafts movements and his output was considerable. His designs included much of the decoration for the Houses of Parliament, several Catholic churches and Scarisbrick Hall in Lancashire. The giant yew standing beside the church was planted shortly after the building was completed.

Leave south along a metalled lane on the west side of St John's. At its end, follow a stone cart-track on the right behind some converted stables and then go through a gate on the left. A grass track drops through the original entrance of the fortification to a stream, the River Leam.

Pause at the bridge to look back and appreciate the effectiveness of Wappenbury's defences. Little imagination is needed to understand the difficulties that would have faced an attacking force armed only with primitive hand weapons. The stone-arched bridge and its functional, although less attractive companion, replace stepping stones that were once the only means of fording the stream. After heavy rains, the crossing was often impassable and prevented people from Hunningham attending church at Wappenbury.

Over the bridge, a trod leads across a field to a gate, keep going ahead along the field margins until, finally, you reach a lane beside the entrance to Hunningham Farm. Turn right, but immediately after a junction, clamber over a stile on the left. Strike diagonally towards another stile at the left-most end of the opposite hedge and then keep going over the ensuing paddocks, making for the church, now ahead. Walk past it on the left to find a yew-lined path leading back through its little cemetery.

In the early thirteenth century, the manor belonged to the Corbicon family, its moated manor house once standing a short distance south-west of the church. St Margaret's was built as a private chapel, but shortly after it was finished, Geoffrey de Corbicon ceded it to Wappenbury with an endowment to maintain a priest because of the difficulties faced by his tenants in crossing the Leam to attend church there. Those dangers of travel remained into the nineteenth century, as illustrated by the death of Wappenbury's vicar in 1819. He drowned whilst trying to cross a flooded ford at neighbouring Eathorpe, although whether the fact that he was 'much intoxicated' had any bearing on the matter is open to conjecture.

The humble building was originally much smaller, consisting only of a small nave and chapel. Periodic repairs were carried out and a new roof added, but by the nineteenth century, it had become so neglected that considerable work was needed to save it from collapse. The western wall is unusual for its buttressing and lancet window and, striking in its simplicity, is the squat weather-boarded belfry. It boasts a weathercock in the finest tradition, but unfortunately it is no longer up to supporting the ancient bells, which now rest on the church floor.

Of interest are boards recording benificious gifts to the poor of the parish. Between 1552 and 1834, poor relief was financed by rates charged on the major landowners. However, the majority of peasants had rights of common and perhaps a small parcel of land to farm and these resources, coupled with a small income, were often enough to ensure self-sufficiency. In winter, sickness or old age, intermittent relief and occasional beneficial gifts helped people remain largely independent in their own homes. However, enclosure and the expansion of industrialisation meant that country labourers became increasingly reliant on waged employment, which was often sporadic and poorly paid. By the beginning of the nineteenth century, poverty in many areas had increased beyond the resources of the parish and the poor came to be regarded as the instrument of their own misfortunes.

Under the 1834 Poor Law Amendment Act, people desperate for relief were required to move into workhouses, where the conditions and harsh regime were deliberately designed to deter all but those in direst circumstances. Described as 'uninviting places of wholesome restraint', families were usually separated and given only the barest essentials to maintain life. In some, inmates had little or nothing to occupy their time, whilst elsewhere, they were set to heavy and monotonous work. In 1846, a poor-house was opened at nearby Hunningham House, but conditions must have been exceptionally severe as it was closed in 1850, following allegations of ill-treatment against the inmates.

Return to the paddock and walk away from the church to a stile in the far left corner, where the River Leam traces its course. Follow the bank upstream, leaving the fields beside an ancient stone bridge opposite the Red Lion inn.

In early times, many river crossings were made at fords, a practice still common until relatively recently. After the departure of the Romans, there was little impetus to build bridges outside towns except to support a few overland trade routes or ease the transit of medieval nobility between their estates. After the Conquest, William had made grants of land to his barons recognising their support. However, being conscious that a single large landholding might make any one individual too powerful, he sought to limit their influence by fragmenting the gifts over disparate areas, thus creating a need for them to regularly move between their various manors. A bridge has existed here across the Leam since at least medieval times but by the seventeenth century it needed substantial repair. Although the work was theoretically the responsibility of the parishes of Hunningham and Weston under Wetherley, the commissioners applied to the quarter sessions of the Knightlow Hundred, in effect the county, for it to bear the cost. The application was successful and the repairs were eventually carried out in 1651 for £20. It remains an impressive structure, resting on massive culwaters which divert flood waters from the supporting piers. The refuges built to allow pedestrians avoid the overhanging loads of carts and pack-horses continue to serve today's walker in a similar fashion.

Over the bridge, the road bends in front of a small pumping station on the left. Just beyond, cross a stile and walk to another at the top right-hand corner of the field. Go on, following the hedge on your left.

The buildings across the fields to the right mark a former reformatory for boys, built in 1840 in what was deemed to be a 'healthy and suitable position'. The inmates, as part of their training, undertook much of the repair and renewal of timberwork within Weston's parish church in 1860. The site was later extended for use as a hospital for mentally handicapped people, but by 1995 this too had closed and the intention now is to build a small housing estate. However, the structure of the original school building and head master's cottage will be preserved.

After a couple of fields, the path switches to the other side of the hedge, eventually bringing you to perhaps the most sensible, if rather unconventional, stile I have yet to encounter. Once over, set a diagonal course to the opposite field corner and then continue ahead beside the hedge, eventually rejoining the road near Weston under Wetherley. The village lies to the right, but the onward route is left towards the church.

The red sandstone church is dedicated to St Michael, who is pictured in the window of the Tower. He is the angel sent by God to cast out Satan and has a parallel in the ancient Persian god of light, who engages in an eternal battle against evil. The saint is often portrayed bearing scales to weigh risen souls seeking admission to the Kingdom. Because of this, he has been adopted as the patron of shopkeepers. Visions of him have been recorded since the fifth century, and in the tenth century, a Benedictine Abbey was founded in his name at Mont Saint Michael in Normandy. Edward the Confessor's chapel at Saint Michael's Mount in Cornwall is reminiscent of that magnificent structure.

There are traces of an original twelfth-century building in two semi-circular Saxon windows in the chancel, but much of the present structure represents later building. The church's oldest monument is a fragment of a woman's hand and dress carved in stone, lying in a small aumbry in the aisle. Her identity is not known, but the size of the recess suggests a child. By a piscina in the chancel's south wall is one of the oldest known brasses in the county commemorating Anne Dunet who died in 1497. Nearly as ancient is its neighbour dated 1566, remembering Joyce Tomer as a physic. One reference to it indicates a man, which is credible in that women practising such arts in those days were likely to be regarded as witches. There are memorials of a similar date in the chapel to the Saunders family, one bearing a quaint rhyme applauding the life of Margerie who died in 1563. The decorated fourteenth-century octagonal font is distinctive in that its faces are alternately flat and concave. Below it depended four carved heads, although one is now missing.

Beyond the church, where the road bends sharply left at Wetherley Lodge, cross a stile on the right and walk ahead along the edge of three successive fields. At the far corner of the third, go through a gap on the left and walk on to a second gap. Beyond that, strike directly ahead across a field, following a northerly setting and aiming for a solitary oak in the far hedge. Maintain the same heading across the subsequent field to reach a gap in a hedge by an indent, part-way along its far boundary. Go through and immediately turn right over a plank bridge, then follow a hedge to the left. At the top, pass through an opening and cross the field corner on the right to a gate. Walk on to the opposite corner, where a stile brings you onto Weston Lane. A short distance to the right, just beyond a large oak tree, mount a stile on the left and walk away. In the next field, a stile on the left crosses to a path leading around the screened perimeter of opencast sand and gravel workings and landfill.

The works in progress have meant that some footpaths are temporarily diverted. The route is liable to slight modification, but any changes will be signed by the County Council.

After passing a derelict windpump, you eventually arrive at a gap in the corner of a hedge.

At one time, such pumps were a more common feature of the countryside and were used to pump water from underground sources to supply isolated cottages or provide drinking water for livestock. Although much neglected, the machinery and pump of this one still remain over the well head.

Pass through and then go left by the hedge towards Bubbenhall House. Before reaching it, pass around to its left and join a track into Bubbenhall Wood. Emerge at the far side over a stile, and make towards Glebe Farm over on the left. Once out of the field, a dirt track leads past its straggling buildings, bending sharply left just beyond. There, cross a stile on the right to another track and walk away from the farm, ultimately returning to the main road on the edge of Bubbenhall.

Although now overtaken by modern dormitory development, there remain one or two interesting cottages and pubs from the older village. The settlement grew here on a low hill above the banks of the Avon rather than around the river crossing, which lies just a little to the west. The site perhaps took advantage of the high ground to avoid flooding and gave its millers the benefit of both wind and water power. The church, at the far end of a cul-de-sac from the main road, is generally closed. Dedicated to St Giles, it was built in the thirteenth century in dark red sandstone.

Walk 6: Henley in Arden, Preston Bagot, Lowsonford and Beaudesert

Although the great forest of Arden, from which Henley took its name, has now gone, the town continues to exude a vitality that has sustained it over the centuries and is one of those rare places that has successfully adapted the essence of its heritage within a changing world. Full of character, the place is worthy of investigation in its own right, but this walk goes further afield to enjoy a landscape that was claimed out of that ancient woodland. After crossing the fields to the south-east, it follows the Stratford Canal which provides a convenient and easy passage through a gentle countryside. The course back is along a disused railway line and a part of the Heart of England Way, returning into Henley past Beaudesert Castle, the 'fine wilderness' described in its name still being appropriate a thousand years on.

Maps: Pathfinder: 975 or Landranger: 151

Start: Henley-in Arden (Map Reference SP 151 660)

Distance: 8¼ miles

Transport: A train service between Stratford and Birmingham stops at Henley Station.

Refreshment: Henley-in-Arden has many attractive eating houses and inns and others are passed near Preston Bagot and Lowsonford.

The bustle of people and passage of traffic have always been features in this busy little place. From early times, it lay on the main route through Arden to the open Feldon in the south and trade was encouraged under the protection of Beaudesert Castle, which commanded the hill behind. In 1140, the de Montforts, whose castle it was, were granted a weekly market and later a fair, and the township grew rich on taxes and profits from trade. Despite being razed about 1268 in reprisals following the de Montforts' defeat in the Barons War, it continued to prosper and, by the middle of the fifteenth century, had been granted a second fair and become largely autonomous. Jurisdiction lay in the hands of the borough

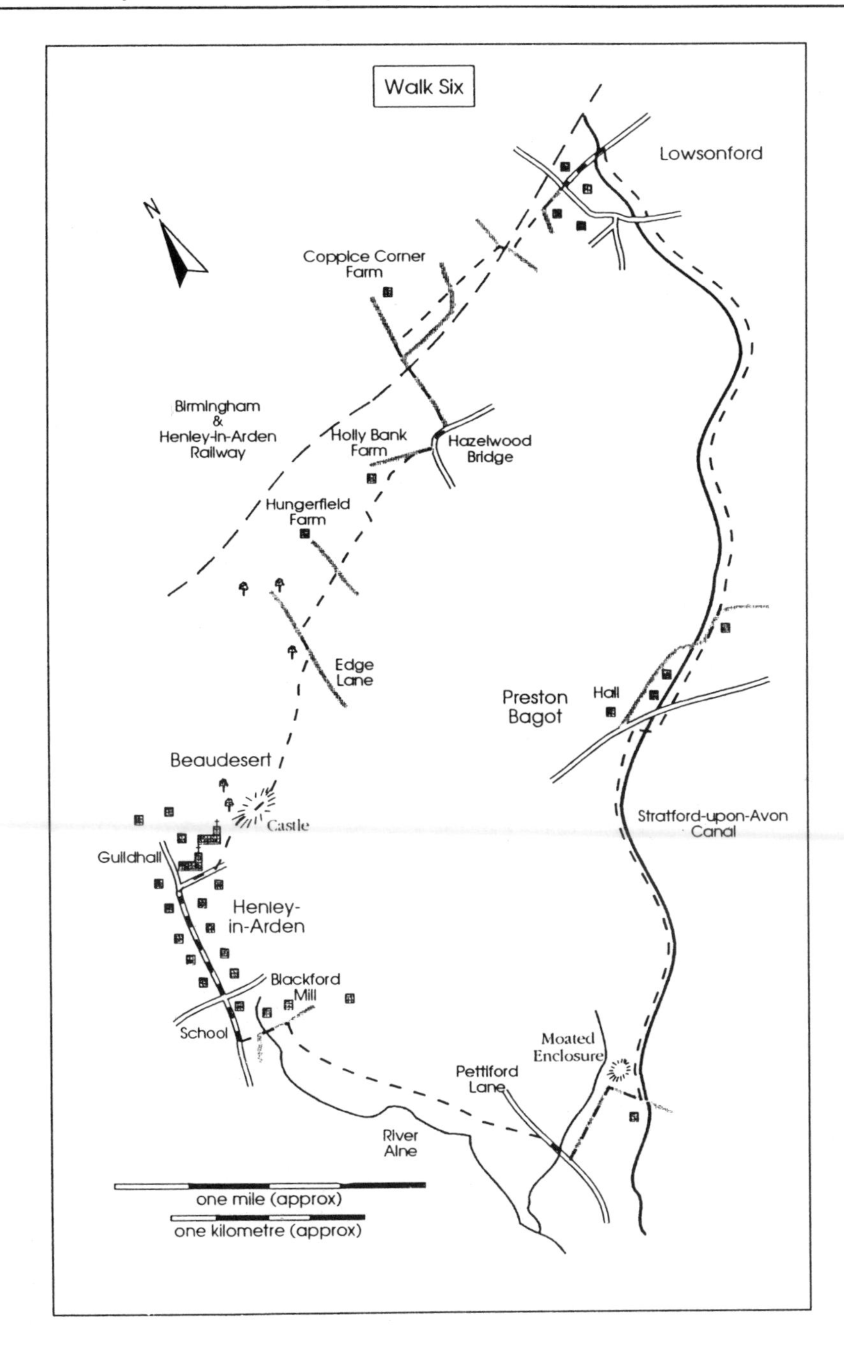
Walk Six
Lowsonford
Coppice Corner Farm
Birmingham & Henley-in-Arden Railway
Holly Bank Farm
Hazelwood Bridge
Hungerfield Farm
Edge Lane
Preston Bagot
Hall
Beaudesert
Castle
Stratford-upon-Avon Canal
Guildhall
Henley-in-Arden
Blackford Mill
School
Moated Enclosure
Pettiford Lane
River Alne
one mile (approx)
one kilometre (approx)

officials rather than the king's sheriff and towns-people had exemption from tolls throughout the realm. In 1725, the road was incorporated within the turnpike between London and Birmingham and a toll house was built on the northern edge of the town. To satisfy the demands made by increasing numbers of travellers, more inns were opened and, by the beginning of the nineteenth century, a third annual fair was established. Although the weekly markets and trading fairs have long ceased, a regular cattle auction still takes place and the high street is always busy with sightseers and shoppers.

Begin the walk by wandering through Henley to appreciate its charms, perhaps pausing to enjoy its justly famous ice cream.

Filled with a glorious mélange of structures from the fifteenth century onwards, oak timbered buildings from three centuries vie with Georgian brick, modern shop fronts fit snugly in late medieval cottages and, although now in need of some support, a fifteenth-century market cross watches twentieth-century traffic pass by.

About half way along the main street, at the side of the guildhall, lies a narrow passage, off which a gated opening leads into a secluded courtyard.

Contained by the mullion-windowed wall of the old guildhall and overlooked by the even more ancient church is a delightful garden wherein stands a mulberry tree, planted to commemorate Queen Elizabeth's Silver Jubilee. More usually associated with the silkworm, which feeds on its leaves before spinning a cocoon, this particular tree is favoured by summer-time wasps who grow drunk on the fermenting juice of its raspberry-like fruits. The fifteenth-century guildhall is particularly interesting. Now serving as the library, it perpetuates the town's tradition of courts baron and leet that still sit here. Amongst the oldest administrative and legal organisations in the country, these were manorial courts established by the Normans to oversee the management of estates and deal with petty crime. Courts baron considered such matters as tenancies, inheritance and the allocation and use of common land

and appointed officials to oversee details of common interest such as the control of wandering cattle, ditch repair and maintain standards in the quality of goods produced for sale. In some manors as here, the feudal lord was also granted jurisdiction over crime, infringements being dealt with by a court leet, a word that came from the French 'eslite', or elected, because of the way in which the officers and jury were determined. This concept of election, which extended to the selection of village officials, gave the feudal system an element of democracy that the ordinary villager did not again enjoy until 1884 the Reform Act, which extended the franchise to country areas. The erosion of the feudal structure and a gradual standardisation of legal and administration systems led to the functions of these courts being superseded and any legal jurisdiction that the few survivors might still have had was finally removed by legislation in 1977. However, many of their principles and functions are embodied within of our modern institutions and the honourary officials of those courts that remain, such as brook lookers and ale, butter, fish and flesh tasters, serve as reminders of the complexities of medieval life.

St John's Church asserts itself over the crush of buildings that surround it by an imposing square tower that dominates the high street. Inside, an array of medieval figures, mythical creatures and a fearsome-looking dragon look down from a splendid roof. Further along, on the opposite side of the street, grandeur on a small scale is a befitting description for Henley's Baptist chapel. Dating from 1867, it suffered a devastating fire in 1936 and was rebuilt the following year.

Go beyond the traffic lights at the southern end of the town and immediately past a speed limit sign, cross a stile on the left into a school playing field. Walk on a quarter-right diagonal to another stile in the far fence and follow the ensuing path over the Alne to emerge beside Blackford Mill. Go left, passing the mill and its attendant cottages before turning into a large field on the right. The defined right of way cuts south-east across the cultivation of successive fields, but custom appears to favour a trod beside the river bank.

Either way, on reaching a meadow, strike a diagonal away from the river, making for a stile in the far corner to the right of a cottage. Go right a short distance along Pettiford Lane and, after crossing a bridge, leave along a tarmac track on the left.

Beyond a bend in the track, the moated enclosure of an ancient manor house is clearly visible in the field on the left.

The track shortly rises to a bridge across the Stratford-upon-Avon Canal.

The Stratford canal has a variety of bridges crossing it, but one that is characteristic of this waterway is the split bridge such as exists here. These were prefabricated in cast iron and consisted of two deck plates cantilevered across the canal from brick abutments on either side. A gap in the middle allowed the towing hawser to pass through, thus avoiding a wider and more expensive bridge spanning both canal and towpath.

The onward route lies along the towpath to the left.

Less affected by the effects of agricultural chemicals and practices, canal-side hedges, banks and copses allow the regeneration of a more natural vegetation. From early spring to late autumn, there is an array of flowers and plants to attract all manner of insects and birds and, if you are lucky, you may also see a fox.

Shortly, beside another bridge, look for a sign attached to an upended length of railway line.

Rather incongruously, the notice, advising of the bridge's safe weight limit, bears the title of the Great Western Railway. It is explained by the fact that canal was purchased by that company in 1856. The development of the railways was strenuously opposed by the canal companies, who foresaw their business dwindling to nothing in the face of competition from a faster mode of transport. In seeking to protect their interests, some companies were able to delay the passage of Railway Bills through parliament whilst seeking to secure some form of compensation. In a number of cases, as was the situation here, outright purchase was negotiated, which returned some benefit to the stockholders. However, few canals disappeared overnight and for many, the construction of nearby railways brought increased traffic for a short while in the carriage of building materials to the site. Although many tried to compete by reducing their tolls, it was only a matter of time before they were finally closed as commercial enterprises.

Presently, Preston Bagot Manor House comes into view. There, before reaching the main road, the towpath crosses to the other bank.

The glow of an afternoon sun enhances the well-seasoned colours in this marvellous old house. Built in about 1550 for the Earl of Warwick it subsequently passed to Ingram Bagot, whose name now identifies the house and nearby village. Close-set timber studding rises from a stone foundation. Displaying all the fashionable characteristics of its day, the walls are infilled with attractive herringbone brickwork and lozenge-section chimneys make an impressive statement of wealth and refinement above the gables of its tiled roof.

Beyond Preston Bagot, the canal climbs through a number of locks beside which stand barrel-roofed cottages, unique to this canal.

William Whitmore, who engineered the southern section of the Stratford Canal, had a limited budget and looked to save money where he could. One of his cost-cutting measures were these utilitarian lockside cottages, built to house the company servants responsible for controlling traffic through the locks. They were all put up between 1811 and 1812 and utilised techniques more fitting to bridge or tunnel construction. The arched roof was formed from a mixture of brick, rubble and mortar and waterproofed with a coating of asphalt.

At Yarningale the canal is taken over a small stream on one of Whitmore's Aqueducts.

Another of the economy measures he employed can be seen in this minimalistic aqueduct, which consists merely of a trough formed from bolted iron plates carried on brick piers. Although this is the shortest of the three he built on the canal and, in fact, is actually a replacement for an original that failed, this bridge adequately demonstrates the simple effectiveness of his solution to what was a considerable engineering problem. Like the split bridges already passed, they were manufactured by the Horseley Iron Company as prefabricated panels to be assembled on site. The other aqueducts lie further to the south, across the road at Wooten Wawen and at Edstone near Bearley Cross. The latter is almost 160 metres long and is second in length in this country only to Telford's aqueduct carrying the Ellesmere canal over the River Dee at Pontcysyllte.

Eventually you are brought to Lowsonford, where the canal passes beneath the road.

Lowsonford was once the home of Fleur de Lys pies, which took their name from the canalside pub where they were made. 'Fleur de lys' actually refers to the yellow flag iris, which Louis VII took as his emblem when he fought in the crusades. It thus become known as 'the flower of Louis'.

Leave the canal for the road at Finwood Bridge, the next one after the pub, cross over the canal and walk on to the junction.

There, on the right is an old cast iron pump. Not that long ago, many villages relied on communal pumps for water. Improvements only came generally from the mid-nineteenth century onwards following a number of public health Acts directed at providing adequate sanitary arrangements and water supplies.

Directly opposite, a track passes between cottages and outbuildings, shortly rising to pass another cottage. There, negotiate a stile on the right into a paddock and cross to a second stile in the far corner. A grass trod then leads, over final stile, to a track. Turn right to go over the remains of a bridge, crossing what was once the line of the Birmingham and Henley in Arden Railway.

The railway was begun in 1860 to connect Henley with the Paddington to Birmingham line of the Great Western Railway at Rowington, but after five years a shortage of capital halted work. Thirty years passed before the work was finally completed by the Great Western and the line was opened in 1894. Later plans for a station at Lowsonford were abandoned with the advent of the 1914-18 war and, in fact, the railway was conscripted. Its metals were taken up with the intention that they would be relaid as a supply line for troops in northern France. Unfortunately, the boat conveying them across the Channel was sunk, and they still rest in their watery grave.

Just beyond the bridge, after mounting a stile, immediately turn left to cross a second stile into a cultivated field. Climb beside a small plantation on the left to the top, where a stile invites you into the trees. The ensuing path drops, shortly emerging in a meadow on the other side. Turn right, initially following the perimeter of the wood and carry on beyond across the next field to meet a track. To the left, it bends around Coppice Corner Farm and ends, through a gate, at another farm track. Go left, carrying on after re-crossing the old railway to a lane at the end.

Turn right, but after crossing Hazelwood Bridge, leave over a cattlegrid along a drive on the right to Holly Bank Farm. A few metres on, beyond a hedge gap, a waymark indicates the footpath forking left off the metalled way and rising to the top left corner of the field. A short distance ahead, another stile leads to a larger field behind the farm. Go half left to join and then follow a hedge to the corner. In the next field, again cross to the far left corner, where the way then lies through a small copse of hawthorn and damson. On emerging, a cleared path bears left of ahead to join an outjutting hedge and carries on to the corner of the field. Cross over a track from Hungerfield Farm into the field opposite and walk to its far left corner, there going left along a grass track, Edge Lane. After a short distance, climb a stile on the right into a meadow and take a left diagonal line to a final stile in its corner.

The ground beyond falls steeply down an open grass bank into the wide, flat valley of the River Alne and gives a fine view of Beaudesert Castle, which occupies the summit of an outcropping spur connected to the main ridge by a lower saddle.

A track runs along the edge of the escarpment to the left and, after passing

over a stile, moves right across the saddle to Beaudesert Mount. The path continues across the summit, where stood the medieval castle, and descends on the far side.

Already defended by the steep flanks of the hill, the castle keep was raised on an artificial mound surrounded by a deep dry moat. Two courtyards lie to the south west, although their defending embankments and ditches are now somewhat obliterated. Its proximity to Edge Lane, which follows the line of an ancient British track above the forested lowlands, suggests that the hilltop may have been defended before the arrival of the Norman rulers. A castle was built by Thurston de Montfort at the end of the eleventh century but it was partially destroyed in 1266 after Peter de Montfort's death at the Battle of Evesham. He had been supporting his cousin, Simon, who led an unsuccessful uprising against Henry III. With the death of the last de Montfort in 1369, the castle reverted to the Earl of Warwick and by the middle of the sixteenth century, it had fallen into ruin. Relics have occasionally been found on the site, for example in 1855, some wooden water pipes were dug up. In their rotting away, holes had appeared in the ground, which had become a danger to grazing cattle causing some broken legs. Despite the lack of obvious remains today, the site is still impressive and is a fine vantage from which the Malverns and Edge Hill can be seen on a clear day.

Dropping along the nose of the spur, the way finally emerges onto a lane through a kissing gate beside the church.

It is unusual to find two parish churches in such close proximity, St John's at Henley lies only a couple of hundred metres away across the Alne, which marks the boundary between the two parishes. This is much the older and there is evidence that a Saxon building preceded the present church. The main construction is substantially of the twelfth century, with the crenellated tower being added in 1448. In the seventeenth century, the roof span was reduced by re-siting the north wall within the body of the church. As a result

St Nicholas' church and Henley from Beaudesert

the fine chancel arch no longer lies symmetrically with the body of the church. The two pointed windows above it, from their position, appear to have been inserted at that time, but unless there was a loft above either the nave or chancel, seem to serve no purpose. The lavish Norman chevron decoration following the chancel arch is particularly fine and is of a similar pattern to that which forms the archivolt above the entrance door and is found over the eastern windows. Splendid ornamentation also embellishes the pillars, capitals and corbels.

The weather vane above the tower shows an image of the saint to whom the church is dedicated, St Nicholas. As Santa Clause, his annual visit is eagerly awaited by children all over the world, but of the man himself, little is known. An early bishop from Myra in Lycia, now encompassed within south-west Turkey, he is thought to have been imprisoned during Galerius' persecution of the Christians under Diocletian at the beginning of the fourth century. However, legends are abundant, all following a pattern in which he intervenes to save trios of people or children from death or persecution. The popular Santa Clause of today developed in the nineteenth century in America from the Dutch Protestant tradition of giving small presents to their children on the 6th of December, the feast day of Sinte Klaas, his name in Dutch.

Follow the lane to return to the main street in Henley.

Walk 7: Haselor, Walcote, Temple Grafton, Exhall, Wixford and Oversley Green

In the east of the county, contained by the rivers Alne, Arrow and Avon, is a land of gently rolling open hills and long escarpments. Despite the area being given mainly to agriculture, there are large banks of woodland that generally follow the lines of higher ground. Our walk is one of ups and downs and to gain the best advantage that the height offers for panoramic views, it is best saved for a fine day. In addition to visiting some of the smaller villages that are characteristic of the area, the circuit passes some of the woods, one of which is managed by Forest Enterprise and to which there is access, and a small nature reserve supported by the Warwickshire Wildlife Trust. The area is also rich in history and a pagan site and Roman road add further dimensions to the expedition.

This longer walk can be shortened by returning by way of Oversley Wood.

Maps: Pathfinder: 997 or Landranger: 150

Start: Haselor (Map Reference: SP 121 576)

Distance: 11 miles (8½ miles for shorter version)

Transport: A sporadic midweek service serves the outlying villages and Oversley is only a short walk from Alcester.

Refreshment: No inns are directly passed, but there are two at Wixford, a short distance south of the church.

Identified on the map as Upton, the village looks to the isolated little church of Haselor across a small valley, whose stream once provided sufficient water to power a mill. Evidence of an early village, a victim to the Black Death, is revealed by hollows in the ground near the church and old field patterns can be traced in the open meadows around. Whilst the depopulation of many villages is often attributed to the plague that devastated the country in 1348 and 1349, the average death rate across the country has been estimated at about 37% of the population. Obviously, there was con-

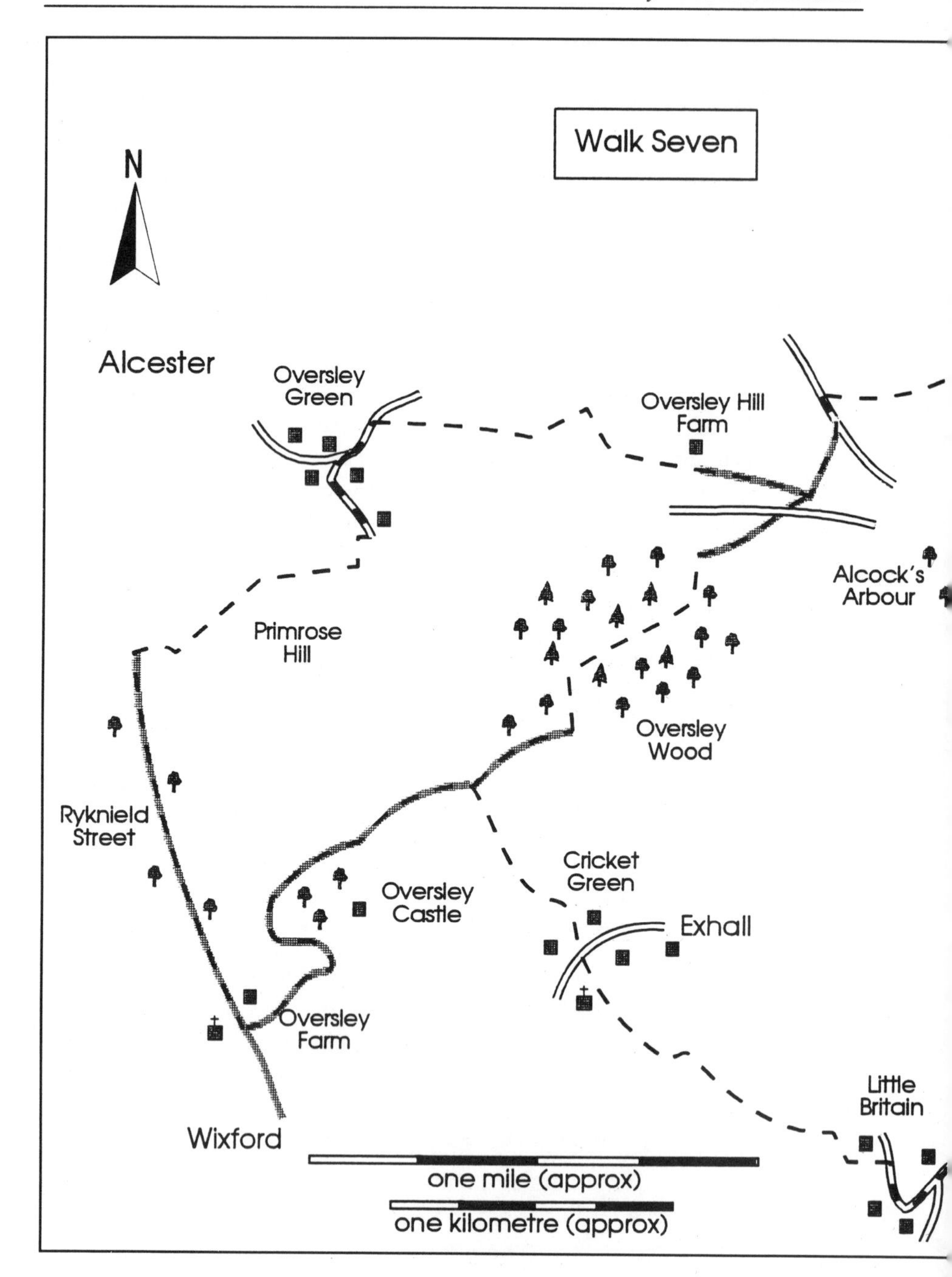
Walk Seven
N
Alcester
Oversley Green
Oversley Hill Farm
Alcock's Arbour
Primrose Hill
Oversley Wood
Ryknield Street
Oversley Castle
Cricket Green
Exhall
Oversley Farm
Wixford
Little Britain
one mile (approx)
one kilometre (approx)

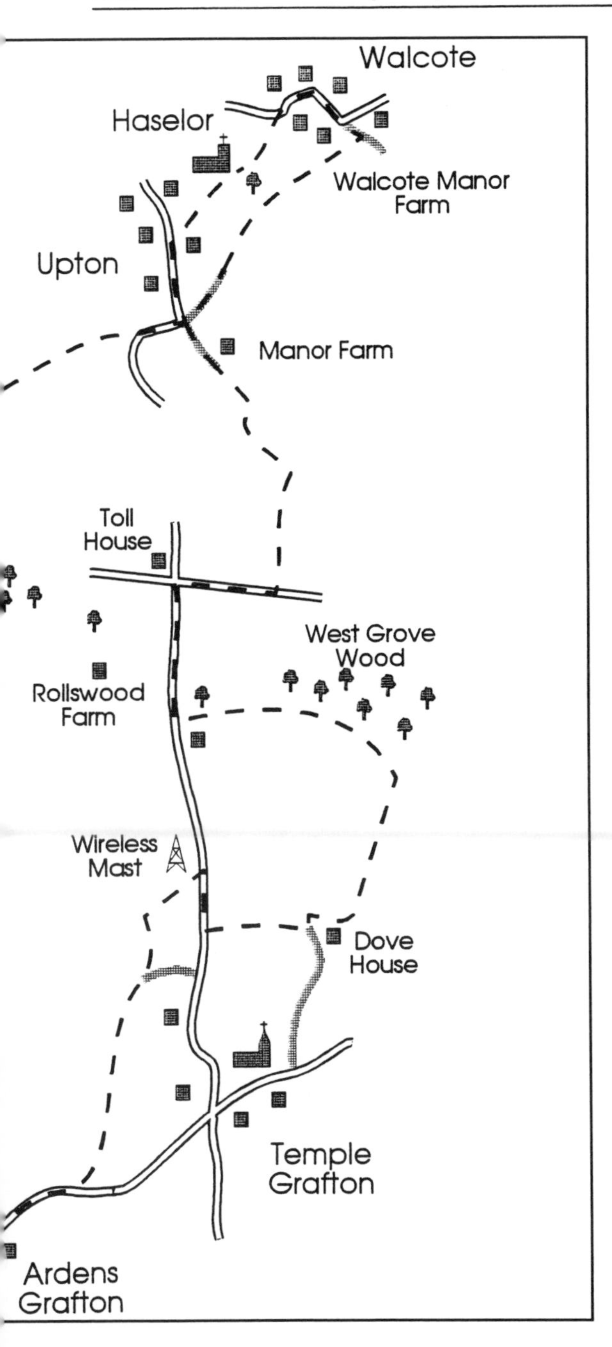

siderable local variation, but in very few places can it be claimed that all the inhabitants perished. Most depopulations would, in fact, have resulted from the survivors moving on to begin new lives elsewhere, either attracted by the new opportunities that a shortage of labour presented or abandoning an area that had become unproductive in any case. The present village contains a delightful mix of timber-frame and brick buildings from the seventeenth century onwards and the old village stocks survive beside the path at the beginning of the walk. The inhabitants must have been an unruly lot in days gone by, as three malefactors could be accommodated together.

Weary returning walkers will be disappointed to find that the inn marked on the map no longer exists. It is perhaps a sign of modern village depopulation, in which expiring leases are sold to the highest bidder, forcing out the local families and the amenities that they supported.

The walk begins from the centre of the village, where a waymarked tarmac footpath leaves the road on its eastern side. Heading directly towards St Mary and All Saints' Church, the path drops to cross a culverted stream and then climbs to enter the churchyard through a kissing gate.

'Haselor' derives from the Old English for hazel-covered hill, on which the church now stands in isolation, giving splendid views over the surrounding countryside. Its origins as a revered site might lie in pre-Christian pagan beliefs and a vague surrounding depression is claimed to be a Druid circle. As many early venerated locations, particularly those on hill-tops or by springs, were absorbed within the new religion, there is some credibility in this belief. A more recent mystery surrounds a weather-beaten headstone near the gate. Its now unreadable inscription referred to the burial of an infant 'near this place', that is, outside the sanctified ground. This was possibly because the child was still-born or born out of wedlock and had thus not been christened. Another curiosity is a small repaired gravestone to Henrietta Matilda, standing to the right of the path beyond the church. A villager returning to Walcote one night, slightly the worse for drink, saw something cross his path in the dark. Believing it to be the devil, he drew a gun and took a shot at it. He might have missed the demon, but he certainly hit the headstone.

The lovely little church, with its low crenellated Norman tower, has been much altered over the years, culminating in major repairs in the nineteenth century to prevent its collapse. The recess on the north wall was built as a mortuary chapel, intended as a resting place for the deceased whilst they awaited burial. One of the walled-up openings is said to be the devil's door, through which the banished spirit could escape during a baptism. In the vestry underneath the tower, a metal plaque records a grant of £65, made to renew the pews on condition that six should be reserved for the poor. Similar notices can be found in many churches in the area. As

Cider press at Walcote

you pass through the wood beyond the churchyard, notice to the left of the path the base of a medieval cross.

Leave the churchyard by a kissing gate at its eastern end. The path passes through a small wood before dropping to join a lane, which to the right, leads into Walcote.

Walcote is a charming hamlet, with several timbered houses. At least one is cruck-framed, that is, the roof being supported on long curving beams rising from the ground and joined at the apex. Whilst this was more economical to build than constructing a jointed frame, the size of the building was limited by the length of log that could be obtained. Generally belonging to poorer cottagers, many were pulled down during the enclosure period and consequently, relatively few have survived. The cider press by the roadside is another interesting rarity. Autumn apples were strewn in the trough and crushed under the vertical wheel drawn round by a horse. Sandwiched between layers of straw, the pulp was then squeezed beneath the large press to extract the juice. After fermentation, the cider was ready to drink, but probably bore little resemblance to today's refined product.

Where the lane bends sharply left at the far end of the village, leave it to walk ahead on a farm track beside Walcote Manor Farm. In about 50 metres, climb a stile on the right and follow the right-hand field edge to the bottom, where a plank bridge leads to a large meadow. Cross to an indented corner on its far side, there meeting an old trackway.

Climbing over the hill beside the church, is an ancient sunken track, which served as a cattle drove and thoroughfare until only three or four generations ago.

Follow it to the left, the hedge on your right, to a gate at its end. Turn right along a lane and at its end, go left on a drive into Manor Farm.

Haselor, Upton and Walcote were once separate demesnes, each with their own manorial seat, this manor house being that of Haselor. The intricate and elaborate brickwork of its chimneys is characteristic of upper-class Elizabethan houses. Previously, even in the homes of the aristocracy, smoke from cooking and heating fires had merely been allowed to escape through the rafters. Improved living conditions and better use of buildings, particularly the division of the great hall into two storeys, brought the concept of a flue and chimney. These very quickly became symbols of status, rising ever taller and incorporating increasingly complex decoration and oversailing. Each house vied with its neighbour to be the most ostentatious. However, the fashion was short-lived and, by the end of the century, it was realised that tall stacks were unnecessary. The classical and continental architectural influences of the following period relegated the chimney to an inconspicuous feature on the subsequent great houses.

Through a gate beyond the farmhouse, a waymarked path carries on past two small barns to follow a hedge to another gate. Keep going with the hedge on your right, through a further gate to the bottom right corner of a field, where there are two more gates. Ignoring that on the right, go through the

one ahead, and walk to the bottom of the field, where a stile leads to a main road. Go right for some 350 metres to a cross-roads and then turn left towards Temple Grafton.

Stratford Road, a former Roman route, was a salt track in medieval times. In 1396, one farmer held his land in return for carrying salt from 'Whiche' (Droitwich) to the manor. Salt was an important commodity, a major use being to preserve the meat killed in autumn, as few cattle could be fed through the winter. The trade is remembered in the old names of two fields by the cross-roads, Great and Little Salter's Piece.

The house on the corner is a former toll-house, one of many that appeared across the country at the beginning of the eighteenth century to control the new turnpike roads. Left to the responsibility of local landowners and parishes, who had neither sufficient finance or authority to effect proper maintenance or improvement, most roads had degenerated into appalling quagmires. The remedy was found in turnpike legislation, which allowed the establishment of trusts with the power to raise money for road construction and recoup their investment through tolls. Engineers like 'Blind Jack' Metcalfe, Telford and McAdam revolutionised road building by introducing surveying and construction techniques that produced the first roads really capable of carrying wheeled traffic to be built in this country since the Romans left.

On the right, as you climb the lane, is Rollswood Farm, and behind, a wooded hill, Alcock's Arbour. At one time, the farm was an inn, infamous as a meeting-place for highwaymen. Of the hill, a story tells that a cave at its base was the haunt of the robber, Alcock. He hid his ill-gotten gains inside, in a coffer secured by three locks and guarded by a cockerel. An Oxford scholar, having found keys to the chest, discovered his den and managed to open the first two locks, but as he tried the third, the 'Cock seized upon him'. The tale continues 'that if one bone of the partie who set the cock there could be brought, he would yield up the chest'.

About 500 metres along the lane, at the top of the first rise, go through a metal gate on the left and walk away on a grass track, from which there is a panoramic view across the countryside back to Haselor. At the far end of the field, go ahead through a gap into the corner of a cultivated field. Turn left and walk along the field edge beside West Grove Wood. Pass through a gap to the next field and follow its left-hand boundary around two sides to reach its far top corner. Wind through three successive gaps, first left, then right and then left again, to end up walking with a tall field hedge on your right gently down-hill towards Temple Grafton. At the end of the hedge, cross to the bottom corner of the adjacent field and turn right, following a waymark along the bottom hedge. Cross a plank bridge to the next field and continue following the left hedge around to the left, eventually coming to a gap in the corner of the field.

To go into Temple Grafton, and thence walk along the lane to Ardens Grafton, go ahead through a gap along a grass way which emerges from the fields to a tarmac track beside Dove House. The track ends at a lane, turn right, passing the church and go straight ahead at the cross-roads. It is then about half a mile to Ardens Grafton.

Referred to in Shakespeare's day as 'hungry Grafton' because of its unproductive land, the description perhaps remains appropriate as it has no inn. From the Old English, 'Grafton' suggests proximity to a pit or trench and indeed quarrying was at one time carried out in the vicinity. It first acquired the prefix 'Temple' in 1535, but the manor may have, in fact, been held by the Knights Hospitaller rather than Templar. Further into antiquity, in 710 the Mercian king, Ceolred, granted the lands to Evesham Abbey, but by mistake named the abbott, a man of questionable character, rather than the house as the beneficiary. To recover the error, a new deed was forged. Grafton claims fame through a licence granted to a William Shakespeare on 27 November 1582, authorising his marriage to Anne Whateley of Temple Grafton. It has been suggested that Whateley was a misreading of Hathaway, but as Shakespeare was a common name, it does not necessarily refer to the Bard. In 1862, the manor passed to James William Carlisle, who demolished the old church, built by the Knights, and commissioned the present one together with his residence, Temple Court, and several other buildings.

In 1944, Grafton narrowly escaped serious damage when a flying fortress involuntarily landed in a field by the village hall. Limping back to base after a raid, its crew had bailed out near Leamington Spa. The pilotless plane, flames streaming from its tail, flew on and although clearing the top of the hill, was brought down by some trees beyond, fortunately missing the nearby cottages and school. Everyone dashed to the rescue, but were scattered when three bombs and ammunition exploded with the heat. Soon American soldiers arrived, who to the disappointment of the souvenir hunters, began removing the wreckage and strings of ammunition festooning the trees. However, plenty of oddments were left and soon re-appeared as an ingenious variety of ornaments and cigarette lighters and part of the cockpit remained lodged in an ash tree for several years afterwards.

Otherwise, turn right and follow the hedge to the next corner, where a stile crosses to a meadow. Walk ahead to a lane beyond a ranch-stile at its far side. Turn right and climb the hill a short distance to a wireless transmitter and go left through a gap in the hedge into a field. Walk diagonally across it, shortly bearing left to join a green track coming from the lane at its bottom end. Turn right and follow it over a low hill, ignoring the crossing path about half way along, to its end where it emerges onto a lane on the outskirts of Ardens Grafton. Turn right and walk through the village, going ahead to Exhall at the junction.

Overlooking a little valley, cutting into a limestone escarpment, Ardens Grafton is little more than an attractive row of cottages flowing with the lane down the hill to the patriotically named Little Britain. It was once the centre of a quarrying industry, producing a quality stone that was valued in Stratford in the fifteenth century, a not inconsiderable distance to transport such a weighty commodity by mule. In 1792, there were plans to construct a branch from the Stratford Canal, some five miles to the east, into the quarries, but the idea failed to materialise and by the middle of the nineteenth century, the industry was in decline.

Leaving the hamlet, the lane bends right, dropping steeply. As the gradient eases, just before reaching a whitewashed cottage, cross a stile in the hedge on the left.

The entrance to a small nature reserve managed by the Warwickshire Wildlife Trust lies a little further along the lane on the right.

Walk ahead beside the cottage and go over a stile in the far fence. Now in a sloping meadow, drop to an indented corner of a hedge ahead and go left along it to another stile. Then, walk diagonally left across a meadow to another stile about half-way along. Once over, follow the hedge on the right to a double stile and bridge. Beyond, keeping the hedge on your left, walk along a succession of field margins towards Exhall, whose church comes into view ahead. Nearing the village, the way becomes a field track emerging by a farm. Keep ahead, passing St Giles' Church to reach a lane.

Before the eighteenth century the village gained the description, 'dodging Exhall', as all roads bypassed it and it was not easy to find. A number of its early sixteenth- and seventeenth-century timbered cottages raised on stone foundations still stand beside the lane. The church shares a dedication to St Giles with that in Cripplegate, London. He was an eighth-century Greek hermit who lived in France. Legend tells that he lived off deer's milk and was wounded by an arrow whilst protecting a forest hind from the king's hunting party. He is consequently regarded as the patron of cripples and nursing mothers. The building, with its unusual belfry, strikingly sheathed in copper, was rather unkindly described as 'exceeding hideous' by William Hutton, in a description of his travels in Shakespeare's country written some hundred years ago. This probably reflected his aversion to the zeal displayed by many of the Victorian church restorers. Some of its twelfth-century origins can be traced in the stone work of the nave and in the doorway and window on the south wall. The simple ball-flower ornament is a beautiful example of early decoration. On the floor by the altar, two small brasses bearing the date 1566 depict John Walsingham, a knight in armour, and his wife, dressed in a pretty patterned gown and cloak. Not visible from the inside, a blocked-up doorway in the north wall still retains its old nail-studded door on the outside.

Cross the lane and follow a short track directly opposite to 'Exhall and Wixford Cricket Club'. Walk beyond the pavilion to the top corner of the cricket field and cross into a meadow. Before you is (or should it be are?) Two Titty Hill. Breast the right mound to reach the top right-hand corner, where there is another stile. Cross this and then a second one, just on your left, into a cultivated field and walk up beside its right-hand hedge. At the crest, the crenellated tower of Oversley Castle appears over to the left and there are extensive views ahead beyond the old Roman town of Alcester, sitting at the confluence of the rivers Arrow and Alne. Drop to the bottom of the field, emerging at a crossing of paths.

> The shorter walk cuts through Oversley Wood, managed by Forest Enterprise, to rejoin the main route across the fields back to Upton. Go right along the marked bridleway skirting the southern corner of the wood. After some 350 metres, where the track turns right to Exhall, go left on a path into the wood to reach a gravel forestry track. Cross it and climb into the trees, rising to a path along the top of the hill. Go right and later take one of the descending paths on the left. At the bottom, turn right along a gravel track, eventually leaving the wood through a gate. Just beyond, turn left through an underpass to rejoin the main walk.

Turn left on a way-marked bridleway and later take the left fork where the track splits. Walk beyond a drive on the left leading up to Oversley Castle and at the next junction after a right-hand bend, go left.

> Oversley Castle was built in the 1800s at the suggestion of the future George IV, to ornament the view across the Arrow valley from Ragley Hall. Ragley lies to the west atop a rounded hill, arboured by a woodland park that was conceived by Capability Brown. The Seymour family began construction of the fine hall, which is open to the public, in 1680, incorporating the ostentatious work of several architectural masters.

The track curves around the western end of the hill eventually to join the main drive from the castle. Turn right. Over to the left, the view is back to Ardens Grafton, which crowns the top of the ridge. The drive finally emerges through painted iron gates onto a gravel track opposite Wixford church, again go right.

> The Domesday Survey shows Wixford having a mill and being a

possession of Evesham Abbey. The fishponds, built beside the river by the monks, are remembered in the name of the nearby Fish Inn. After the Dissolution, the manor passed in 1541 to Sir George Throckmorton, with whose family it remained until the beginning of this century.

St Milburgas' church overlooks the ancient Roman road called Ryknild Street. In a corner of the churchyard is an ancient rustic hut, its wooden walls clad in gorse and roof recently re-thatched with straw. At one time it served as a stable for the rector's horse. Nearby stands a massive stepped pedestal and stump of a fifteenth-century cross and embracing the path within its massive spreading branches is an antediluvian yew, standing since at least the sixteenth century. The building dates from the eleventh century and was lengthened in the thirteenth century. It has an attractive south porch and wooden belfry topped by a shingle-covered spire, erected during restoration work undertaken in 1881. If it is open, go inside to look at the grand marble table tomb and magnificent brass of Thomas de Cruwe and his wife. Lawyer to the Countess of Warwick, he died in 1411 and is depicted resplendent in full armour. His wife lies beside him, more delicately attired and accompanied by her dog. Nearby are other brasses to Rise Griffin a child 'but three-quarters old' and the fruitful Jane Alline and her ten children.

The track follows the Roman road north past Oversley Farm, rising in the fields beyond to give a view across the River Arrow to Ragley Park. As we expect from Roman roads, it runs more or less straight and is intermittently bordered by trees. Ignore the two crossing farm tracks and walk to its end at a way-marked gate by the main road. Go right along an open field track beside a cultivated field.

Ryknild Street ran some 60 miles from Bourton-on-the-Water to Wall near Brownhills, where it met Watling Street. Although this particular section is now a green lane, it served as the road to Alcester until 1785 when the present road, running along the west bank of the Arrow, was laid by Viscount Beauchamp. The now dismantled railway, also running beside the river was opened in

1866 by the Evesham and Redditch Railway Company. The station at Wixford closed in 1950 and the line itself disappeared in 1962.

A gate and stile lead to a meadow, the onward path following the left-hand hedge. To the right rises the partly wooded, steep bank of Primrose Hill, which in spring fully justifies its epithet. Walk to the far end and cross a stile on the left to the wide verge of a main road. Walk on to a foot-bridge, using it to cross the road. The path beyond drops to Primrose Lane, which leads into Oversley Green. Turn right into Mill Lane and walk through the village, going right again at its end onto Stratford Road.

Oversley Green, although without church or inn, has happily retained its traditional red telephone kiosk and a Victorian letter-box. Despite its proximity to the ever-developing Alcester, it has remained a separate hamlet, probably protected by the intervening twists of the River Arrow.

In about 200 metres, immediately past a double field gate, leave along a waymarked footpath on the right. The path follows a brook, overhung with pollarded willows. At the end, keep going across the bottom of a paddock, a golf driving range (beware of flying golf balls!) and then a field. At the far corner, ignore a stile on the left, instead, turn right along the bottom edge, heading in the direction of Oversley Wood. Go through a gate and then immediately cross a stile into a meadow rising to Oversley Hill Farm. Climb up the field beside a rough hedge to pass a corrugated barn. There, a field track develops and leads out of the field at the top, continuing as a fenced track to a junction by an access tunnel under the main road, through which the short-cut rejoins the main route.

Turn left and follow the track to a main road. Again go left, but almost immediately, cross a stile into the field on the right. Walk up its right-hand edge to the top corner where a gate on the right leads to the adjacent field. Turn left, the right of way continuing to follow the hedge over the hill, but periodically swapping sides as dictated by waymarks. Eventually you are brought to a track that shortly, after passing through a couple of gates, ends at a lane. Walk ahead, following the lane left around a bend to return to Haselor.

Walk 8: Hoo Mill and Kinwarton Dovecote

It is a great pity to miss Hoo Mill and the dovecote and church at Kinwarton, which, although close to the last walk, cannot be conveniently included within a circular footpath walk. However, even on their own, they make a delightful short stroll and provide an ideal opportunity for a picnic beneath the gracefully flowing willows that here line the banks of the Alne. Although the shortest walk in the book, it should not be missed.

Maps: Pathfinder: 997 or Landranger: 150

Start: Layby on the Walcote to Alcester road about 1¼ miles west of Walcote (Map Reference: SP 108 576)

Distance: 1¾ miles

Transport: The start of the walk is about 1½ miles from Alcester

Refreshment: Bring a picnic

A few metres west of the layby, turn right along a narrow lane, signed to Hoo Mill. Part-way down, the lane bends right towards the mill.

> In a setting that Constable would have appreciated, the mill (a private property) stands at the edge of a pond, which is separated from the main run of the river by a leat lined by ancient pollarded willows. A weir contains the pool, from which the water is channelled to the wheel, housed in the end of the old mill building. A mill has stood here since at least 1086, although its present name seems to have been adopted from 1609. In 1844, it was run by Holyoake of Redditch to power a needle mill, whose business had formerly been carried out from Oversley Mill, about one-third of a mile west of Oversley Green. Together with nails, guns, linen and gloves, needle-making was one of the area's main industries. All these trades had started as cottage occupations that contributed to the village's farming economy before the large scale agricultural enclosures and advent of the industrial revolution.

Retrace your steps to the bend and then go right, dropping to the River Alne.

Those with an adventurous spirit might try crossing the ford, but there is also a footbridge to a meadow on the opposite side. Once over, walk to the far side of the field, and go through a gate to a track. It bends right by Shepherd's Cottage, and then continues ahead, passing Glebe Farm to Kinwarton Church.

All that remains to mark the old hamlet that nestled in these flood meadows is a Georgian brick rectory, the seventeenth-century timber-framed Glebe Farm and a beautiful little church, hiding in a clump of trees. Evidence of an earlier church is found in the shaft of a cross standing by the path, dated to around 900, but the present building is of late thirteenth-century construction. Surviving the nineteenth-century rebuilding, the windows in the south and north walls date from various periods. Of particular curiosity is the middle one in the south wall, as it has a sub-frame of oak and is thought to date from the 1500s. The font well pre-dates the church and has staples and a bar by which the lid could be locked. Before the Reformation, holy water was consecrated only once a year and

St Mary's Church, Kinwarton

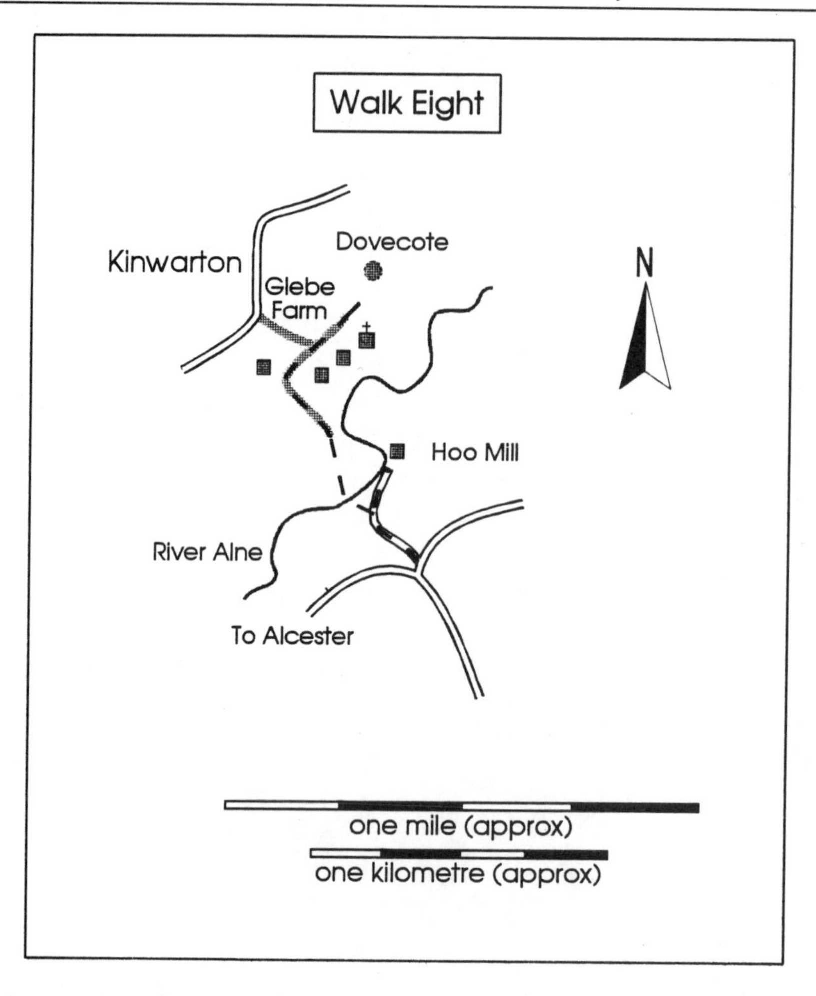

in a superstitious community, it was regarded as having great power. Consequently, it formed an ingredient in many 'black magic' spells and was liable to be pilfered. Also not to be missed is a small, finely carved alabaster panel portraying the Dedication of the Madonna. It was found, perhaps fittingly, in the shavings of a carpenter's workshop in 1836. Thought to be medieval, it would have formed part of a set and be mounted in a wooden frame to serve as a reredos.

The dovecote, cared for by the National Trust, lies in a field just beyond the church. A key can be obtained from Glebe Farm.

A plain circular building, of rendered stone and capped with a conical tiled roof, the dovecote was built in the fourteenth century and attached to a moated manor house that used to stand nearby to the north. Dovecotes were the sole prerogative of medieval manorial owners and their flock of birds ensured a supply of fresh meat during the lean winter months. The practice was despised by the peasants, for not only were they denied the pleasure of the meat, but further suffered because the birds grew fat upon their field crops. As you enter, mind your head, but notice the elaborate ogive arch above the door. Inside, the 600-odd nesting boxes lining the walls were reached from the potence, a ladder attached to a central revolving spindle. A further benefit to the owner came with the rich manure that accumulated on the floor over the years.

Return by the outward route.

Walk 9: Wellesbourne, Newbold Pacey, Ashorne, Wasperton, Hampton Lucy and Charlecote

To the north-east of Stratford, the meandering Avon has carved a wide swathe through the rolling landscape. Its eastern bank rises only gradually, giving the countryside an open aspect where occasional small plantations and hedgerow trees stand as prominent features. This rather longer walk, beginning for ease of accessability on the outskirts of Wellesbourne, explores some of the smaller villages interspersed upon the higher ground above the river vales. It then drops onto the flood plains to return past the exceptionally fine hall and deer park at Charlecote. Nevertheless, it is not a demanding walk and there are plenty of distractions encountered along the way.

Maps: Pathfinder: 998 or Landranger: 151

Start: Kings Head on the B4086 at Wellesbourne (Map Reference 277 556)

Distance: 9¾ miles

Transport: Wellesbourne is served by bus from Stratford.

Refreshment: There are inns at Ashorne, Hampton Lucy, Charlecote and, of course, Wellesbourne itself.

Straddling the River Dene, this busy little town now combines Wellesbourne Hastings and Wellesbourne Mountford. They originally evolved as separate medieval manors either side of the river and in spite of modern developments, attractive corners can still be found. In the late 1960s, the river sought to again separate the two settlements when it overspilled its course after heavy rains, flooding parts of the centre of the town to a depth of five feet. St Peter's Church, to the rear of the Kings Head, was much restored in the nineteenth century, but retains a Norman arch on the north wall of the chancel. It is unfortunate that it is usually closed, as there are fine stained glass windows, one depicting the Apostles coming from the 1875 London Exhibition and some beautiful mosaic work by the alter. It also contains a fine small fifteenth-century brass of Thomas le Strange, one time Constable of Ireland.

Wellesbourne entered history in February 1872, when an address was given by Joseph Arch to a meeting of discontented farm workers outside the Stag's Head. Throughout the nineteenth century, farm labourers had suffered increasing hardship from changes in farming practice, fluctuating markets and an increasing dependence on an industrialised market economy. Many labourers left the land for the expanding factories or to emigrate to the 'new' countries. For those that remained, working conditions were arduous, regular employment was uncertain and wages, even when supplemented by poor funds, were barely sufficient to maintain a family in summer let alone through the harshness of winter. At the beginning of the century, workers' combinations were illegal (as, incidentally, were those of employers) and demonstrations, threats and riots had been met by harsh punitive measures, transportation and occasionally execution. Although the combination laws were repealed in 1824, lack of organised leadership had left farm workers largely impotent in improving their conditions. Arch, himself a farm worker from nearby Barford, where he is remembered in the name of the village pub, emerged with a determination to change the situation and his training as a Primitive Methodist preacher helped him become a competent leader and organiser. He travelled Warwickshire's villages encouraging co-operative action, which, at the Wellesbourne meeting, culminated in the formation of the Warwickshire Agricultural Labourers' Union under Arch's leadership.

He achieved almost immediate success in increasing labourers' wages to 2s 8d (about 13 pence) a day following a short strike. More importantly, he gained national publicity and support for his cause and, by the end of May, escalating enthusiasm led to the formation of the National Agricultural Labourers' Union to which Arch was elected president. It quickly attracted a considerable membership and, although only lasting for twenty-four years, it

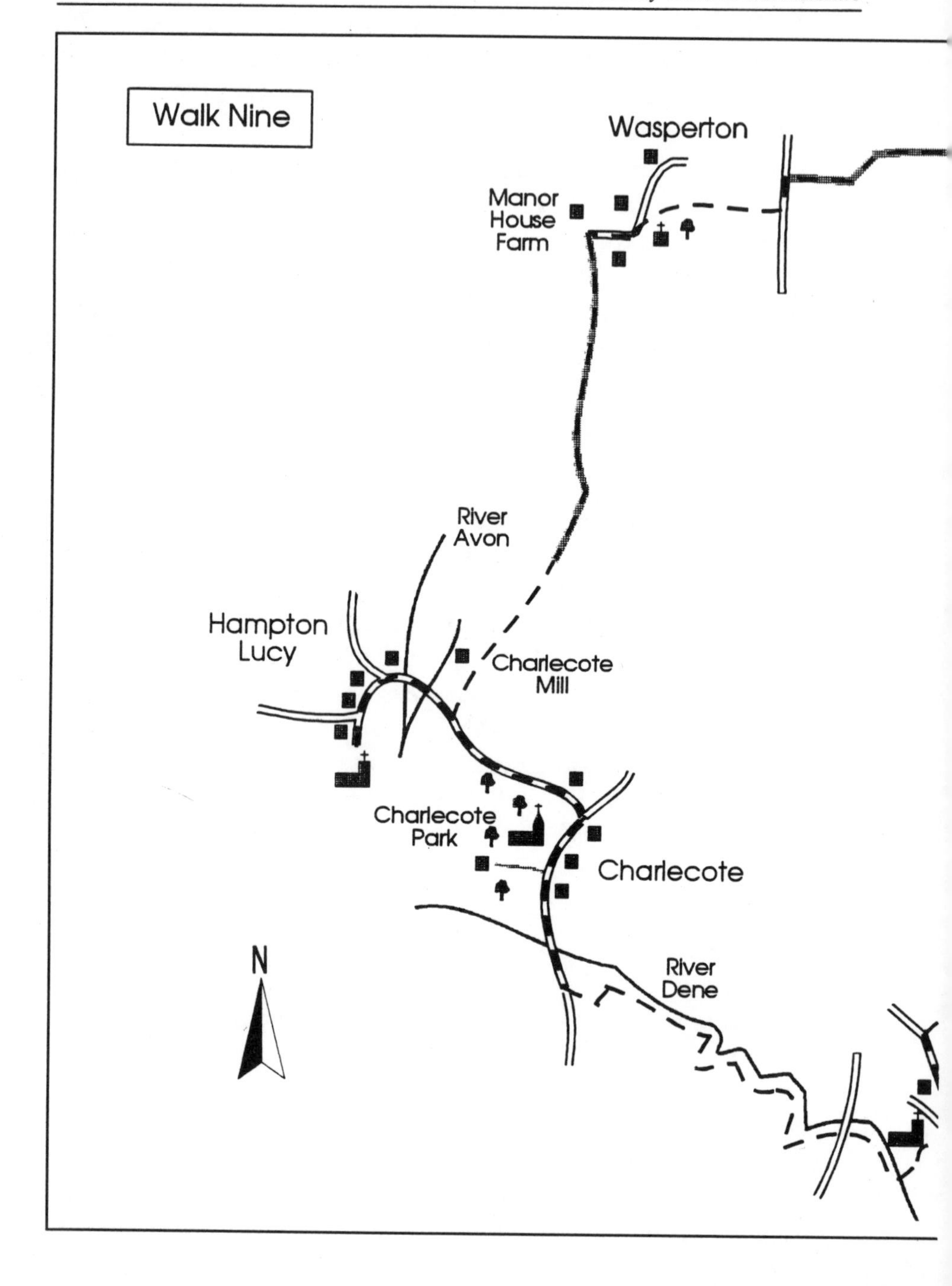
Walk Nine
Wasperton
Manor House Farm
River Avon
Hampton Lucy
Charlecote Mill
Charlecote Park
Charlecote
River Dene
N

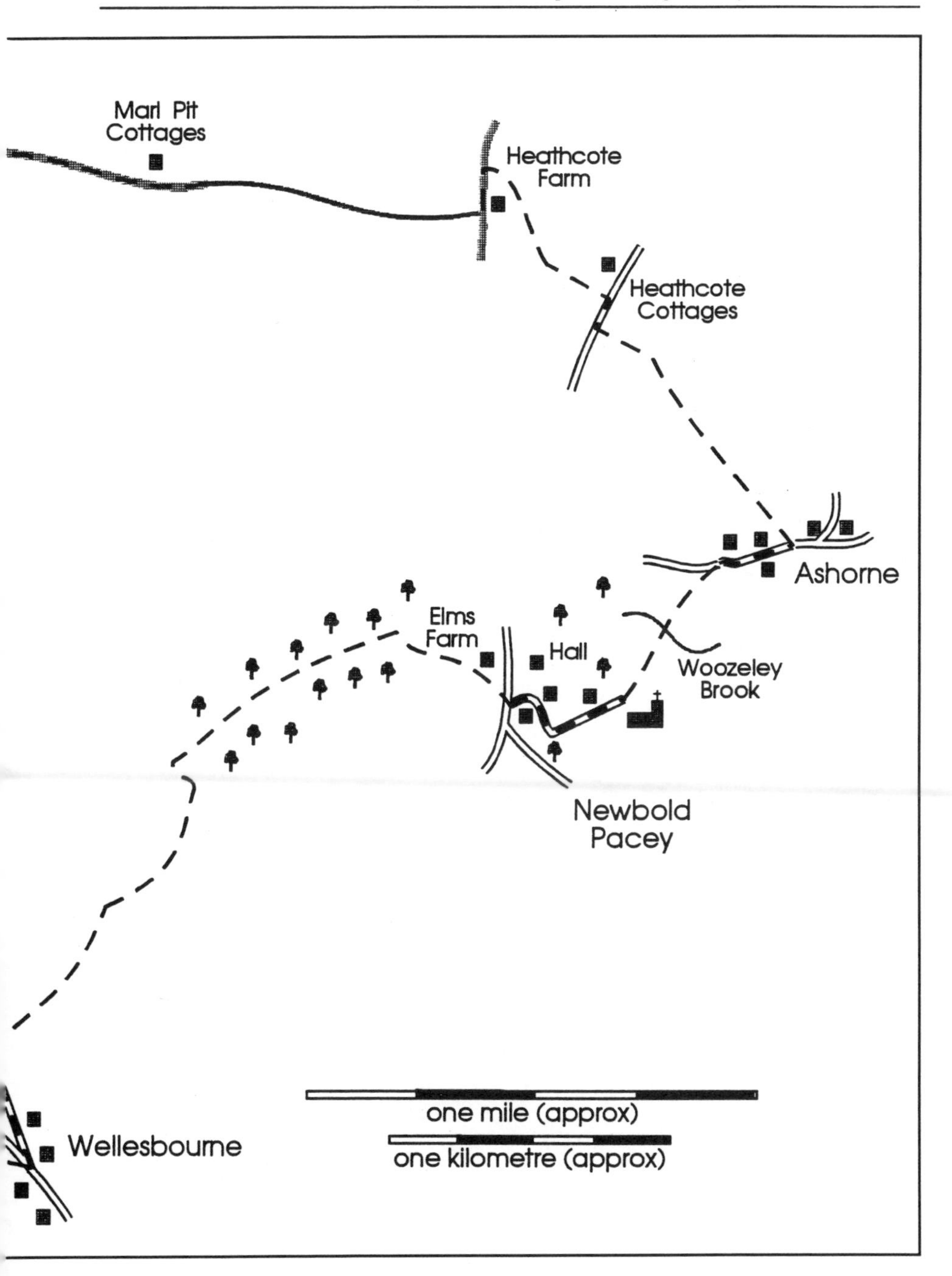
Marl Pit Cottages
Heathcote Farm
Heathcote Cottages
Ashorne
Elms Farm
Hall
Woozeley Brook
Newbold Pacey
Wellesbourne
one mile (approx)
one kilometre (approx)

achieved much, not least in its pressure to extend franchise rights to rural workers. This contributed to the Liberals being elected to government in 1885, Arch securing the seat of North-west Norfolk. It is perhaps ironic that the first farm labourer to enter Parliament, in representing Sandringham, had the Prince of Wales as one of his constituents.

Begin the walk along Warwick Road, a cul-de-sac opposite the Kings Head. Where it is barred by a gate, pass through a gap into a field on the right and follow its left-hand hedge, eventually crossing a culverted stream. Walk directly ahead to the far corner of the next field, and through a gap, follow an overhead powerline and subsequent short fence to go through another opening. Go on, initially beside the hedge on the right, but where it later bends away, keep ahead to pass through a gap at the far corner. Follow the hedge ahead up the field, shortly turning right at its corner beside a strip of woodland. After about 50 metres, enter the trees to find a grass track winding through the spinney. Further on, after briefly emerging from the trees beside the edge of a field, it reaches a clearing from which a track on the right leads to a lane at Newbold Pacey beside Elms Farm.

Newbold's epithet derives from the De Pasci family who held the manor in the twelfth century and, until the early fourteenth century, a small village encircled the church. It disappeared as the result of enclosure in about 1327, when the hovels were pulled down and the peasants removed to Ashorne. Scant evidence remains in the humps and hollows of the surrounding fields. The manor house has also long since gone, but in its place is an eighteenth-century stucco hall, its design attributed to Wyatt. It lies back from the road behind trees, presiding over spacious parkland and can be glimpsed later in the walk.

A sign at the start of a narrow lane opposite marks the way to the church.

A couple of estate cottages and a timber-framed house bearing a Victorian post-box line the lane to the church. The village's original eleventh-century church was destroyed by fire and the present building was erected in 1880. Its stark outward appearance is emphasised by a saddle-back tower and is a marked contrast to

Charlecote Hall

the interior, particularly the roof, which is supported by an intricate pattern of timbers. The narrow aisle is dominated by a massive 'tortoise' stove that proclaims 'slow but sure combustion' and there is a rather touching seventeenth-century monument to Felicia Carew, who died in the 'thirteenth day of her age'. The reredos depicts Saint George, to whom the church is dedicated, victorious over the dragon. He is thought to have been a Roman legionary who was beheaded around 303 in Palestine for his Christian beliefs. His legendary victory over the dragon, in which he saved Cleolinda, the King of Silene's daughter, from sacrifice to appease the beast which was terrorising the city, symbolises the conquest of good over evil. St George was adopted as the patron of soldiers after he appeared in a vision to the Christian army in 1098 before a victorious battle against the Saracens. In the fourteenth century, he was embraced as the patron saint of England.

Leave the far end of the churchyard into a meadow and cross to a gate at its

top corner. Carry on along the field margin, Newbold Pacey Hall lying across the parkland to the left. After crossing a small brook, climb to the top right corner of Ashorne cricket field. Leave through a wrought iron gate onto a lane and turn right to the village.

> The meandering stream at the bottom of the cricket field is rather quaintly known as Woozeley Brook and separates the cricket field from its pavilion, which lies within Newbold Pacey. The little village above is very attractive, a charming row of thatched timber-framed cottages standing beyond the Cottage Tavern.

Just before the street forks by the cottages, leave along a waymarked concrete track on the left. When it bends left, walk ahead up a low bank to a grass track and carry on between allotment plots, through a gate and then over a stile to a field beyond. Walk ahead up the first field and then directly across the second, making for the third tree from the left on the far boundary. Keep your bearing over the next two fields, leaving by stiles near their far left corners, finally reaching a ridged meadow. Cross that on a left diagonal to a gate in the middle of the far hedge and turn right onto a lane beyond.

Before reaching a small layby, leave through an opening in the hedge on the left and walk away from the lane. Towards the end of the field, cross through the hedge into the adjacent field and keeping to its boundary walk around to the second, far corner at the bottom. A short grass track then leads on to a gate, but ignore it, going instead through a waymarked gap on the right. Cross the next field diagonally to the far corner of Heathcote Farm and, through a gap, turn left along the field edge to reach a tarmac track. Now, head left past the farm, and turn right onto a grass track opposite the entrance to the farm house. The route across the fields is in no doubt, go straight ahead at a junction and, about two-thirds of a mile after Marl Pit Cottages, you will reach a main road just east of Wasperton.

Opposite, to the left, a grass track leaves through a gate. At the far end of the field, where it bends right to rejoin a road, walk ahead to a stile and cross the drive beyond to an enclosed footpath. A little way along, look for a discrete metal kissing gate in the hedge on the right. A narrow path then winds through the trees to a cemetery, where a yew-lined avenue leads to St John the Baptist's Church.

Sadly the little church is often closed, but if you time your passing to coincide with a service, inside you will find a wrought iron communion rail, decorated with birds holding sprigs of mistletoe. The pulpit is also of interest, incorporating a series of early eighteenth-century carved panels that depict John the Baptist, Adam and Eve, Abraham and Issac, Jacob and Charity. The church was rebuilt in 1843 by Sir Gilbert Scott, who was perhaps the most celebrated of the Gothic Revival architects. His work was prolific and included humble village churches, like this, as well as grand edifices such as St Pancras Station and Glasgow University. Its style is of the fourteenth century and its rather plain exterior is countered by an unusual belfry exposing the bell carriage and an attractive timbered porch.

Leave by the main entrance, following a road left to its end at Manor House Farm. There, again turn left along a dirt track across the fields which later passes an angling pool before ending by some newly planted trees. At that point, walk right on a green track around the edge of the plantation and carry on past a rough enclosure. At the far end, a path on the left leads through a gap to a gated bridge. On the far side, go through a gate on the right into a rough meadow and walk diagonally across, heading for the almost cathedral-like silhouette of St Peter's Church at Hampton Lucy. Keep going over the next two meadows, leaving through a gate in the final corner to join Charlecote Road. Turn right and walk over the Avon into the village.

On the Avon's west bank, Hampton Lucy is an agreeable village, its old centre being near the church. To its west, presiding over a tiny green is the Boar's Head and nearby are some timber-framed and thatched cottages. There are also some nineteenth-century estate cottages, whose neatness impressed a traveller of that time. The monks of Worcester were granted the manor in 781 by the Mercian king Offa, and it remained with them until 1549. Known as Bishop's Hampton, the present suffix was only acquired after the lands were granted to the Lucy family in 1557. As was usual in the middle ages, tenancies were agreed in return for a combination of rent and service and it is recorded that in 1182, peasants here were required to work for the feudal lord for three days each week. They spent the remaining days either in looking after their own farming interests or perhaps gathering fuel from the surrounding heath and woodland. At that time the village farmed a two-field system, the fields being known as Netherfelde and Overfelde. There was also a common pasture, lying to the south of the village in the crook of the Avon, its identity being kept in the name of Old Pasture Farm. An open heath area to the north-west is similarly remembered by 'Hampton Gorse' and 'Gorse Cottage'. The process of clearance and enclosure began towards the end of the thirteenth century creating sheep walks and by 1480 the settlement at Hatton, which lay just a little to the west, had been completely cleared. In Hampton, a more piecemeal approach was adopted with the last enclosures occurring only about 1740. Fewer evictions took place here and left sufficient inhabitants to volunteer, with men from Wellesbourne and Loxley, to form a local militia in preparedness against a feared Napoleonic invasion in the early nineteenth century.

St Peter's Church, at the south-eastern corner of the village, is a grand building and splendid palingenesis of the Early English style. From the elegant body of the church rises a magnificent tower topped by four slender spires, which stands as a distinctive landmark for miles around. It was an early design of the Gothic revivalist architect Thomas Rickman and commissioned by the Reverend John Lucy, rector here for almost 60 years until his death in 1874. After demolishing the original thirteenth century church, building began in 1822, taking four years and £23,000 to complete. Later, under the direction of Sir Gilbert Scott, the beautifully detailed apsidal chancel and north porch were added. The external elegance is perpetuated inside in the windows, a carved alabaster font, choir stalls and a small area of fourteenth-century floor tiling at the western end of the south aisle. Near the front of the church, a framed copy of the rules of the Hampton Lucy Clothing Society is displayed. They exemplify the high moral tone often adopted towards the poor by charity trustees, who demanded discipline, subservience and soberness in return for the meagre support provided.

Retrace your steps along the lane by which you entered the village, continuing along it towards Charlecote.

The lane leaves over two bridges. The first, spanning the Avon, was funded by the Reverend John Lucy and cast at the Horseley Iron Works, famous for the standardised bridges produced for the Midland canals. The second crosses the tail of a mill race from Charlecote Mill, the not inconsiderable brick edifice half hiding behind the trees upstream. It houses two waterwheels powered by separate races that pass beneath the building.

At the end of the lane, turn right and walk, first past the church, and then the gated entrance of Charlecote House and park.

The small village stands opposite the house it was built to serve, separated by an expansive park laid out to the design of 'Capability' Brown in 1760. Previously, the road had passed much closer to the house, but to secure privacy, George Lucy had it removed to a more discrete distance. The Lucys can trace their history here to the twelfth century, when the estate was acquired by Thurstane de Cherlecote. The Lucy name was adopted in about 1247 by his great grandson Sir William, who married a daughter of the de Lucy family of Cockermouth. Thomas Lucy, the first of three successive Lucys to bear that name, built the hall in 1551. It is regarded as the first example of Elizabethan architecture, although much of the original fabric has suffered alteration and rebuilding in subsequent ages. The Lucy family still live here and gave the house and some 200 acres of park to the National Trust in 1945. It is open to the public during the summer months.

There is much to see in the park, an avenue, once of elms, leads to an Elizabethan gatehouse, an exceptional and rare survival from that period. Built of brick and dressed in stone, a pierced balustrade and flanking towers provide simple decoration to this beautiful building. Beyond, that original decorative refinement is repeated in the house, due largely to George Hammond Lucy's careful rebuilding in the nineteenth century, which recreated its original Elizabethan style. He was the brother of the Reverend John Lucy, who you remember, built the church at Hampton Lucy. Inside, the rooms are exquisitely decorated and furnished, whilst outside, the stables, a wash house and brew house vividly portray some of the less glamorous practicalities of life on a large estate.

St Leonard's Church was the inspiration of George Hammond's wife, Mary Elizabeth. After her husband's death, she continued making improvements to the house and estate and conceived the church as a family memorial. She had the original twelfth-century building demolished and work commenced on the new church in 1850. The heaviness of the vaulting adds to the impression of darkness of its interior, but this is gently dispelled by light filtering through impressive east and west windows. Your attention cannot fail being drawn to the magnificent effigies of the three Thomas Lucys contained in the little north chapel. Taken from the earlier church, they are fine examples of the funerary statuary of their period. The first Thomas, who built the Elizabethan house, lies in effigy on the right with his wife Alice attended by two of their children, shown kneeling in the end panel. On the left is the second Thomas, with his wife Constance kneeling before the tomb in prayer. His fourteen children, from two marriages, line the front panel. Perhaps the most striking, because of its flamboyant style, although separated in time by not that many years, is the canopied Carrara marble representation of the third Thomas and his wife. The books he loved in life are shown about him and, although his death was due to a fall from his horse, Thomas' enthusiasm for riding is depicted in a panel.

Beyond the park, the road crosses the River Dene, a tributary of the Avon. Just after, turn left onto a farm-track and then go left again to follow a signed path along the river-bank. The meanderings of the river are emulated by the path, wandering upstream towards Wellesbourne. Eventually the route passes underneath the ring-road and along the edge of a meadow, finally bringing you a footbridge over the river. The path beyond leads into the churchyard of St Peter's Parish Church. The Kings Head, from where you began the walk, lies at the other side of the church.

Walk 10: Wolfhampcote, Flecknoe, Shuckburgh and Braunston

Rising amongst the western hills of Northamptonshire, the River Leam's early northern course marks the boundary between the two counties before immersing itself within the Warwickshire countryside. Although not high, the gentle hills that overlook its infant passage command expansive views across the countryside, which on a good day, extend as far as the Welsh hills. This prominence made them ideal for early settlement, when the lower lying land was heavily forested, but by the time the Romans arrived, the area was largely agricultural. In fact, the region's name 'Feldon' derives from the Old English term feld or open, cleared land. This walk takes advantage of the high ground in this rather remote corner of the county in an excursion that includes a landscaped park, small hamlets and vanished villages. The return route is by the Oxford Canal, which runs to the once important canal junction at Braunston, just across the county border.

Maps: Pathfinder: 977 or Landrangers: 151 & 152

Start: Wolfhampcote Church (Map Reference SP 529 653)
For those arriving by public transport, Braunston presents a more convenient beginning. A track to Wolfhampcote leaves the A45 where it crosses the Grand Union Canal (Map Reference SP 535 659).

Distance: 8¼ miles or 9¼ miles including Braunston Junction

Transport: Nearby Braunston is served from Rugby and Banbury.

Refreshment: There are inns at Flecknoe and Braunston but you may find a picnic more convenient.

From at least Saxon times until the end of the fifteenth century, Wolfhampcote and its neighbour Braunstonbury, supported thriving peasant communities who cultivated the surrounding fields. However, medieval trade brought a rapid expansion in the export of worsted goods and an increased demand for wool and many landowners, anticipating large profits, turned their estates over to

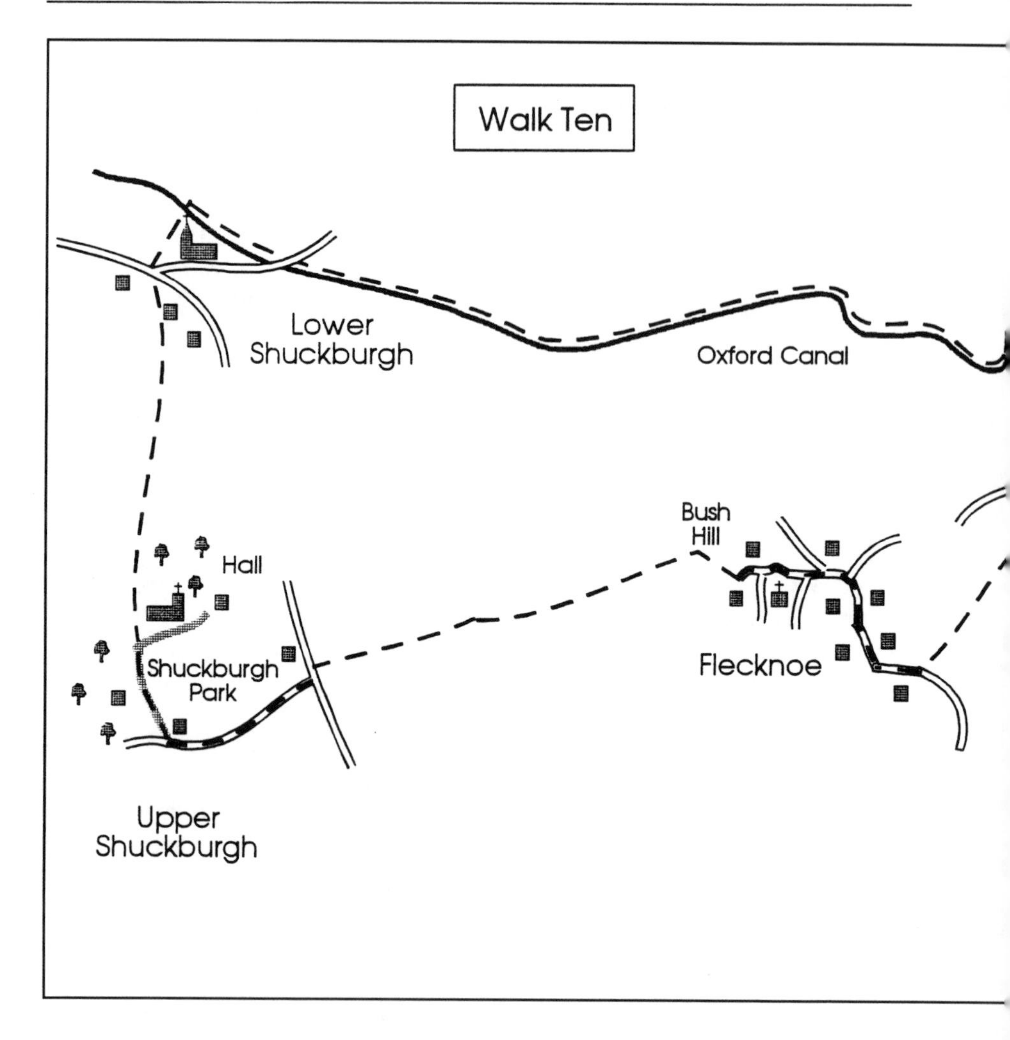

sheep runs. In 1501, these two villages went the way of many, the tenants were evicted and their cottages cleared. All that remains today are a few low mounds and hollows, the ridges and furrows of the ancient fields and a lonely church.

Sheltered by a few trees and surrounded by ancient gravestones, many now too weathered to decipher, St Peter's Church is a rather plain building, its low sturdiness emphasised by a diminutive crenel-

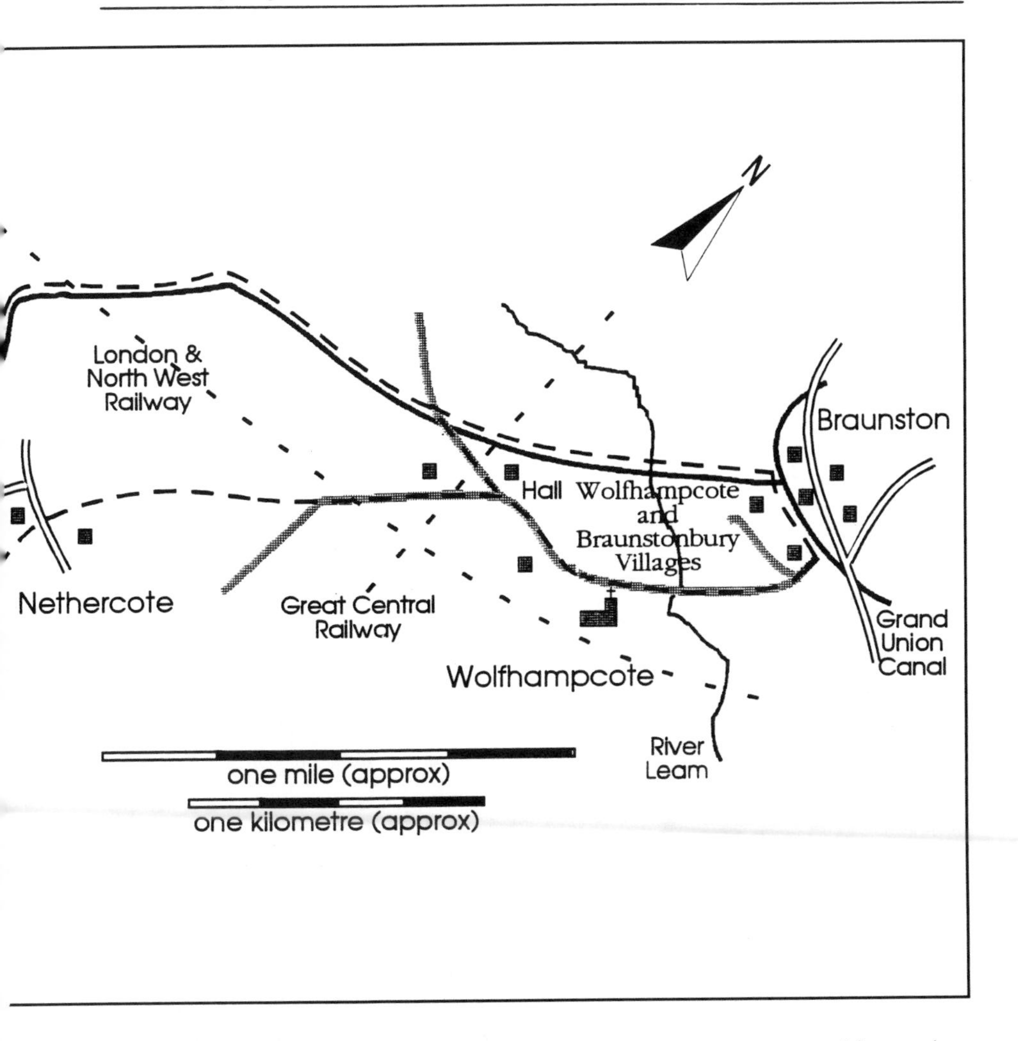

lated tower. No longer used for regular services, it is cared for under the Redundant Churches Fund. Ask at the nearby cottage for a key which opens a door in the south wall of the choir. In the nave are a number of benches from the fifteenth century, they are rather low and of unusual design, one having carving on its end panel. At either side of the chancel arch are carved heads and above are displayed the Arms of Queen Anne. Amongst the gravestones on the floor is a brass plate inscribed for the wife of a one-time vicar, Thomas Benyon, and set in the floor of the south chapel is an ancient coffin lid. Until 1952, the tower held two bells, one of which now hangs in the little church at Flecknoe. Some idea of the effort taken to ring them is conveyed by the large bell-carriage wheel displayed on the tower wall. Other relics include an old chest, a funeral bier and, possibly a link with its Saxon origins, a primitive un-ornamented font.

Walk west along the lane away from the church.

When first built, the Oxford Canal looped around Wolfhampcote and, near the hall, the lane crosses its original line. Opened in 1790, Brindley's canal took a meandering 91 miles to join the Coventry Canal to the Thames at Oxford. However, in response to competition from the Grand Junction Canal in 1827, plans were formulated to straighten some sections and thus decrease its length by 14 miles. In the end, a reduction of only 11 miles was achieved, with one of the

The Grand Union Canal at Braunston

more significant improvements being made here at Wolfhampcote. Previously, the canal curved around the Hall before meandering south, eventually to cross the River Leam. It then returned north to join what is now the Grand Union Canal, just east of Braunston. In all, some 2½ miles were saved by taking the canal over the river on a low three-arched aqueduct. The 'ponds' by the side of the path are remnants of that old loop.

Further on, you cross the former railways of the London and North West and the Great Central companies, their derelict embankments, cuttings and bridges now echoing only intangible memories of steam's golden age. Although important routes, both had closed by the mid-1960s after little more than a hundred years' operation. A plan has recently been put forward to reinstate the track between Nethercote and Wolfhampcote as part of a scheme to create a high speed freight link from the Midlands to the Channel Tunnel. Although having the potential to remove a considerable amount of traffic from the roads, the plans have so far been rejected by the Government.

Where the track eventually bends sharply to the left, leave the road and keep ahead through a break in the hedge on the right. Walk to the end of a hedge on the left and then turn left, crossing to a wide gap in the opposite hedge. Now make for a gate, to the right of the house ahead and then cross the next meadow to another gate in its far right-hand corner. Once through, turn left and follow its boundary to a lane at Nethercote. Go left a few metres before crossing into a paddock on the right at the corner of a high brick wall. Now, walk ahead across a succession of fields towards the buildings of Flecknoe, eventually emerging in the village and turn right. Follow the street past the Old Olive Bush pub and then go left at the next two junctions, ahead then stands the plain brick chapel of St Mark's.

Rising up the flanks of Bush Hill, Flecknoe is a pleasant little village mixing modern houses, eighteenth-century vernacular brick and earlier mullion-windowed stone cottages. Although extensive enclosures took place here in 1744 and 1757, they did not have the same drastic depopulating effects as had been experienced at Wolfhampcote. The long lines of hedgerows fanning out to the south of the village were planted at that time to mark the newly created fields.

At the side of the village pump, the unpretentious red-brick church of St Mark was built in 1891, interestingly at a later date than the Methodists who dedicated their tiny chapel in 1837.

Turn into Bush Hill Lane, passed on the right just before reaching the church. Beyond a bend at the top, take a track on the right, which passes through a farm to the fields behind. Keep going, the hedge on your right, down the far side of the hill to pass through an opening. Cross a field to its far right corner and then walk to a break beside an ash tree in the opposite hedge of the next field. Now following the left hedge, continue across the fields, eventually crossing a ditch and then climbing to emerge at a road. Opposite, to the left, is a drive into Shuckburgh Park. Follow it as far as the lodge gates and go through, climbing on the edge of the park past the rambling buildings of Home Farm. Towards the top of the hill, where the drive bends towards the hall, strike off ahead to an enclosed wood, in which lies a church to St John the Baptist.

A herd of deer roams the tree-studded park, overlooked by Shuckburgh Hall. Its hill-top site gives a fine view across the Leam valley to Northamptonshire and in the opposite direction, the Welsh mountains can be seen on a clear day. Although apparently a Victorian mansion, the house evolved from a much older timber-framed hall, the stucco front being built in 1844. The seat has been held by the Shuckburgh family since the twelfth century and is said to be one of the longest continuous family possessions in the country. One of the earliest references concerns Robert de Shuckburgh. During the uncertain years of Steven's reign, when his cousin, the Empress Matilda, daughter and accepted heir to Henry I, tried to gain the throne to which she should have succeeded, Robert's daughter was forcibly carried off by Warin de Walcote. Warin, a 'knight errant', effectively an outlaw, was eventually captured and executed and Isabel, now with a son, was able to return to her father. In 1660 Charles II bestowed a baronetcy on John Shuckburgh in recognition of the support that his father, Richard, had given to the Royalist cause during the Civil Wars. Richard had fought alongside Charles I at Edge Hill and was later wounded and captured whilst defending Shuckburgh against the Parliamentary forces. He was only released after payment of a large ransom. In contrast to these swashbuckling events, the family name received quite a different honour when it was bestowed upon a small lunar crater, remembering Sir George Shuckburgh-Evelyn who was something of an astronomer in the eighteenth century.

Of the medieval village of Upper Shuckburgh, little remains. The parish, together with its counterpart, Lower Shuckburgh were largely enclosed in the early sixteenth century, and the land put to pasture. The remainder was enclosed in 1778 and the greatly reduced population became focused on the lower village. The little church, originally of the twelfth century and once attached to Wroxall, contains many Shuckburgh family memorials, including amongst the tombs and effigies, one with an astrolabe and globe for the family's astronomer. Unfortunately, it is not generally open. On the outside, curiously incorporated within the north-east wall is a coffin lid. The south-east wall is inset with stones macabrely carved with a skull and cross-bones, said to have come from Esher Mansion.

Retrace your steps from the church through the scissor stile and double back right, joining a track dropping beside a power transmission line on the opposite side of the hill. Go through a gate in the deer fence and head towards Lower Shuckburgh, its church now visible ahead. The way descends a broad grassy ridge to a ditch, from which a grass track passes behind a pair of cottages to a couple of gates. At the far corner of the meadow beyond is a main road and opposite, a short track passing by the side of the church.

The meadows around the church, also to St John, are distinctly ridged and indicate the extent of the old farming patterns that existed before the enclosures. The present church dates from 1864, replacing a thirteenth-century building with a low-tower, nave and chancel. Although also generally closed, its exterior is nevertheless interesting. An unusual Moorish influence embellishes the often mundane Gothic style adopted for so many Victorian churches, the design being inspired by George Shuckburgh's experiences in the Crimea. The use of yellow stone contrasting against grey lias, a scalloped gable with a double-arched entrance, arches, window tracery and mosaic work set it apart from its contemporaries.

Cross the meadow behind the church to a footbridge over the canal and join the towpath on its far bank.

The verges of this section of waterway are delightfully unkempt, and there is a profusion of wild flowers and other plants growing at the waterside and beneath the accompanying hedges. The Oxford Canal was one of the early Midland canals and engineered by the pioneer Brindley. The project was authorised in 1769 and took twenty years to complete, creating a route from London via the Thames to the Midlands and thence to the north-west and north-east, which gave considerable impetus to the industrialisation of the region. The sinuous route, although reflecting a conservative approach to the engineering problems created by an undulating topography, also brought the canal and its advantages to many more villages and farms than would have been served by a more direct route. As with Brindley's other Midland canals, it was constructed to the narrow-boat gauge both for economy and to minimise water use. This section, between Napton and Braunston, was only widened after it had been incorporated within the Grand Union in the 1930s. The canal lost its monopoly in 1805 when the Grand Junction arrived at Braunston from Brentford creating a preferable route that avoided the problems of the lengthy and difficult Thames Navigation. However, this short section linking Braunston to the Warwick Canal at Napton provided a short-cut into Birmingham compared with the otherwise protracted detour via Coventry and Fazely and thus continued to generate high revenues.

It is some 3 miles along the towpath to Wolfhampcote, but the way is easy and passes through a pleasing gentle countryside.

About 140 metres before you arrive at bridge 98, the line of the original canal can be seen on the left through the trees, where a short section remains in water as an angling pond. The line crossed the present canal about 450 metres further on as it headed south in search of a suitable crossing of the Leam.

Leave the towpath and join a track over the canal at bridge 98, continuing across the open grazing beyond. Shortly, it rejoins the outward route near Wolfhampcote Hall.

If you have the time and energy, you might continue along the canal for about another mile, crossing the Leam to Braunston Junction.

The aqueduct over the river, marking the boundary between Warwickshire and Northamptonshire, appears more as an embankment from the canal, but gives an excellent view across the abandoned sites of Wolfhampcote and Braunstonbury. A little further on lies Braunston where, anticipating today's ubiquitous roundabout, the canal junction incorporates an island across which the towpath is carried on a triple bridge. The outer sections are of cast iron and manufactured at Horseley Iron Works. These bridges were mass-produced as prefabricated 'kits' to be assembled on site and were a distinctive feature of the northern section of the Oxford Canal when it was improved in the 1830s. From 1880, Braunston developed into a strategic junction, on which traffic from all the country's major industrial centres converged. Going left, the Oxford Canal continues to Hawkesbury to meet the Coventry Canal and right, the canal passes through the 1,850 metre long Braunston Tunnel to Buckby, where it again divides to London and the north-east Midlands. A feature of the canals, particularly at an important junction such as this, was a company office, often attached to a house, from which a clerk would record the cargoes and tonnage and collect the necessary tolls. They might, like many of the canal-side inns, also provide stabling and horse feed. The one here has its own walled garden, privy and stables.

To return to Wolfhampcote, turn right at the junction, following the

Grand Union only a short distance before leaving the towpath at the next bridge. Immediately on the right, a track signed to Wolfhampcote Church drops past Castle Cottage to open meadows. Where it shortly divides, take the left fork and keep going to Wolfhampcote, about two-thirds of a mile further on.

Walk 11: Priors Hardwick and Wormleighton

From the western edge of Berry Hill, the vast catchment of the River Avon and its tributaries stretches to the sunset. Stratford lies some 18 miles away and the high ground to the south-west forms the Dassett Hills. Since medieval times, the area has grown rich from the woollen and cattle trades and even today, much of the land remains in pasture. Small villages and farms are scattered amongst the rounded low hills, their mellow buildings formed from the beautifully honey-coloured limestone which underlies the soil. The two villages encountered in this walk contrast in their character, one rambling and the other more formally laid, whilst nearby buried under the fields, are the remains of two earlier settlements.

Beginning from St Mary's Church in Priors Hardwick, the walk climbs the hill above the village before dropping to cross the fields to Wormleighton. The return follows the towpath by the Oxford Canal and in all, but for the short initial pull, is a relaxing walk.

Maps: Pathfinder: 999 or Landranger: 151

Start: St Mary's Church in Priors Hardwick (SP 471 562) – note that the Butcher's Arms car-park is for patrons only.

Distance: 6¼ miles

Transport: No convenient services are available.

Refreshment: The Butcher's Arms in Priors Hardwick

A handsome village, its name betraying its history as a priory's livestock farm. It was one of twenty-four manors given to support the foundation of a monastery at Coventry by Leofrike prior to the arrival of the Normans and remained with it until the Dissolution. The village had more than its share of hardship, first being decimated by plague and later, towards the end of the sixteenth century, again depopulated when Richard Blount enclosed the manor to put it to more highly profitable sheep farming. As you follow the walk, you will see that sheep still form an important part

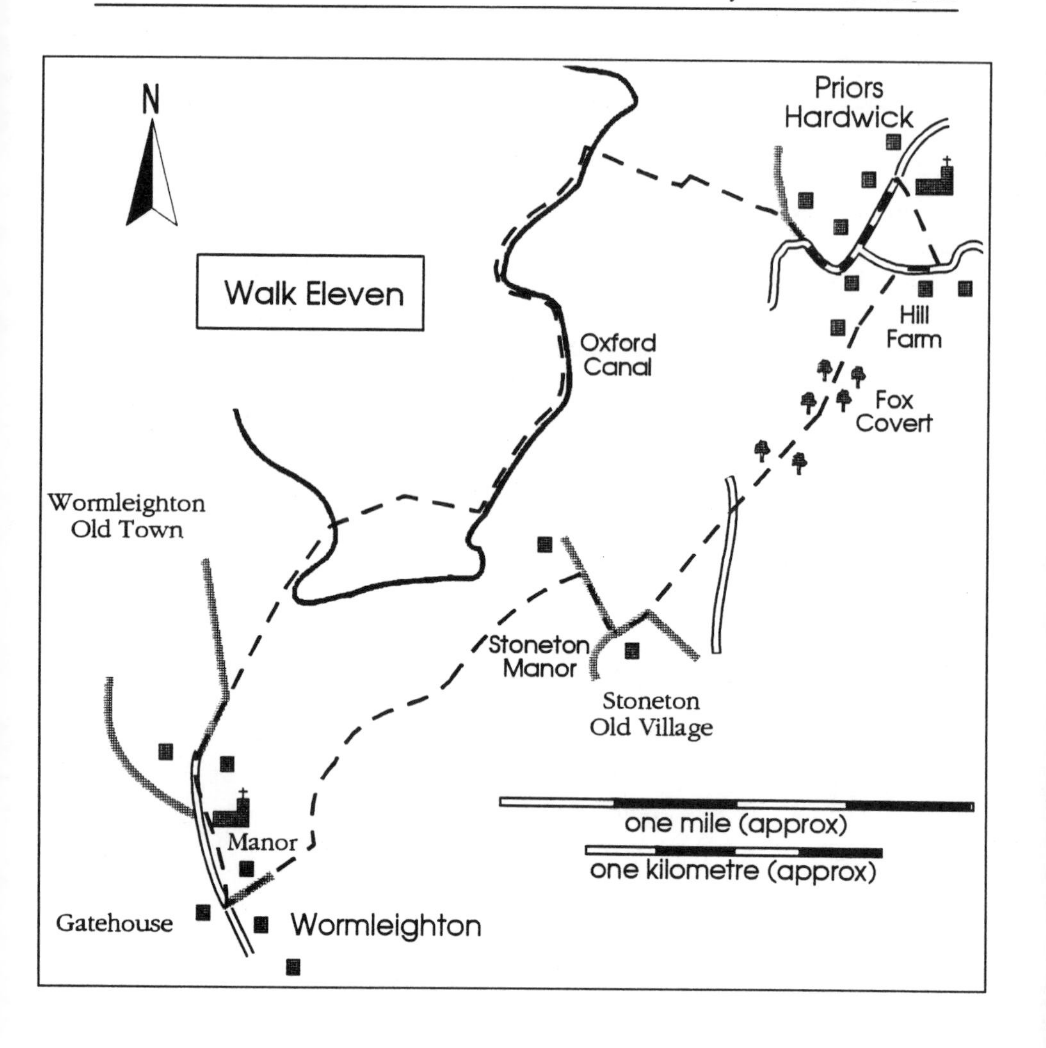

of the economy and, as much of the land has remained in pasture, the distinctive humps and hollows of the older strip agriculture have been preserved.

St Mary's Church is a lovely old building surrounded by trees, its soft mustard-coloured Hornton stone a perfect foil for a setting summer sun. Parts of the square embattled tower and chancel go back to the thirteenth century, but there was much rebuilding in the 1860s. In its cool interior, look up to see the carvings of Paul, Peter, Judas and others amongst the angels. Set in the floor of the chancel is an incised alabaster grave slab, depicting a fifteenth-century armoured knight, his feet resting upon his faithful dog.

A field path leaves the southern corner of the churchyard over a stream, climbing up to a lane in front of the Old Vicarage at the far side. A little way to the right, just beyond an attractive thatched stone cottage and opposite Hill Farm, cross into a meadow on the left. Climb up it, heading half right and aiming just left of a house appearing on the skyline at the top of Hardwick Hill. Go through a gate at the top and walk ahead, maintaining a line roughly parallel with the top of the steep scarp.

The hillside gives an opportunity to enjoy impressive and extensive views over the surrounding countryside. The Oxford Canal is just visible to the right in the near distance, as it meanders to the south.

Ahead, the way enters Fox Covert and takes an easy course through the trees. At the far end, keep following the hedge through a field gate. A little further on, where the right boundary turns down the slope, bear half right down the hill to skirt the bottom edge of more woodland lower down. Find a stile and pass through the narrow belt of trees into another field beyond. Keep going diagonally down the hillside to the road, heading for a stile near a tree in the bottom hedge. On the opposite side of the road to the left, cross another hedge stile and strike diagonally left across the field, making towards the farm buildings of Stoneton Moat Farm. There, leave the field to join a tarmac drive from the road and follow it towards the manor.

Stoneton is an unpretentious manor house in a lovely setting. Its moat, restored by the present owner, derives its water from a spring in the hillside below which it nestles. There has been a house here since the tenth century and the small estate once belonged to a knight. Towards the end of the sixteenth century it passed with Priors Hardwick to the Spencers of Wormleighton. Beyond the house near the road, some low humps and hollows in the field are all that remain of Stoneton Village, which was cleared in the Middle Ages.

Before the drive turns to cross the moat, pass through a wide gate on the right and follow the dropping farm track towards some barns. Just before you reach them, strike off to the left through a double field-gate (way-marked) into a large cultivated field. Walk ahead on a broad track, a Permissive Footpath by agreement with the owner, passing through three gaps into successive fields. Part way along the edge of the fourth field, ignore the wide gap in a shallow corner and keep following the field edge which subsequently bends to the left. Shortly, you arrive at a second gap through which a track bisects the open fields, running directly to Wormleighton, whose buildings are now clearly visible behind the trees. At the far end, go over a stile and across a small paddock, finally emerging beside the manor house in the hamlet.

The boundaries of the manor were settled in Saxon times and a village with a moated manor house once stood at the bottom of the hill near where the canal now runs. Visited by famine and plague, it was finally razed in 1498, by William Cope, cofferer to Henry VII. His interest was in the wool trade and he cleared the village and

Cottages at Wormleighton

enclosed the fields to create profitable sheep grazing, evicting some 60 people in the process. In 1506, he sold the manor to John Spencer for £2,000. Some six years later, following complaints against the enclosure, Spencer was ordered to return the land to open cultivation. In his defence, he pointed out that what he had paid for the estate reflected the increased value of enclosed land and also that in fact he employed as many people as had previously worked the land. He also listed a new manor, improvements to the church, tree planting for fuel and fattening cattle for the London market as benefits gained by the enclosures. He must have won sympathy, but as a concession built 12 cottages, attaching some land to them. The sheep farming continued to be profitable, and at one time, the family were reputed to be the wealthiest in the land.

Much of Spencer's fine manor house, enhanced by successive generations of the family, has sadly disappeared. It had served as a base for Prince Rupert before the Battle of Edge Hill, but was later fired by the Royalists to prevent it falling to Cromwell. Only part of a wing now remains, although that is not insubstantial and vestiges of its imposing features are still evident. Still complete is the imposing arched gatehouse, built in 1613 from golden ashlar. It incorporates a low tower and lodge and carries in its decoration the arms of the Spencers and James I.

Turn right, walking past what is left of the manor house away from the gatehouse and take a path to the church.

Set amidst tired and gently leaning gravestones, is St Peter's Church, another creation from the attractive Hornton stone. Dating from the mid-twelfth century, it probably replaces an earlier wooden structure. Later additions are the thirteenth-century tower and aisles and an extension to the chancel. The striking rood screen was brought from St James' Church at Southam to prevent it being destroyed during Cromwell's puritanical purges. Notice also the little carving of a bespectacled head on the left. There are more lovely wood carvings and panelling in the chancel. We cannot leave without remembering the village's connection with George Washington, America's first president. In 1608, his great-great-grand-uncle, also George, was christened in the font by the door.

A gate to the north of the church returns you to the lane, which leads past some cottages and barns to become a field track. However, before leaving the barns, walk a short distance down a bridleway on the left, where a view over the hedge can be had across ancient field patterns to the site of 'the old town', the cleared village. Rejoin the track to drop gently between open fields, giving a fine view ahead. A little way down, fork right along a lesser track to the Oxford Canal. Keep going to the bridge and cross over.

The ridge to the south of Priors Hardwick, along which you began the walk, now lies half-right ahead.

Walk directly away from the canal on a grass track ahead, following the hedge. Keep going across the next field and in the third field, go half right from the gate to regain the canal by a bridge. Turn left and follow the towpath for about a mile to the next bridge, number 124.

Although the vegetation along the canal banks is periodically cut back to maintain the path, the minimal management encourages a wonderful variety of spring and summer flowers. Notice also the recent layering in some sections of the hedge. As well as acting as boundaries, hedges were used to control livestock, but left unchecked, they grow tall and leggy, allowing animals to push through. However, by laying the stems diagonally, an impenetrable barrier is created. Different regions evolved their own styles and the Midland form, developed primarily to contain cattle, is sometimes called a bullock fence. After clearing the side growth, layering involves partly severing and bending selected stems or pleachers back over a line of stakes placed behind and parallel to the hedge-line. The pleachers are then held securely in place by stems of ash, hazel or willow, twisted rope-fashion across the top of the stakes. A thinner arable version places the stakes along the centre line of the hedge. So finished, with proper maintenance, it can be fifty years before the job needs repeating.

Cross over the waterway and walk away beside the hedge across a distinctly ridged meadow. Half-way along, at a dog-leg in the hedge, cross through a gate to its other side. Carry on beside the hedge to the top, leaving for a track. Follow this to the right past the farm and keep going ahead when it joins a lane. At a fork, go left to return to the middle of Priors Hardwick, passing the stone-built Butcher's Arms.

Behind the pub is an extensive garden, which patrons of the restaurant can visit at appropriate times during the year. There is also a general charity open day during the summer.

Walk 12: Ilmington

Settled in the Cotswold fringe, Ilmington is full of character, not least portrayed in the well-seasoned hues of its stone buildings which are accentuated by the glow of low sun. An evening stroll through its twisting lanes and alleys, beside walled gardens and past charming cottages is a pleasure to be savoured. This walk, however, encourages you further afield, to explore the undulating countryside that surrounds it, although nowhere are the hills unduly steep such as to deter even the un-energetic walker. The ancient elms that gave the village its name may now have gone, but many trees remain, providing shady corners and wooded banks and add so much interest to this varied landscape. Whilst the walk passes one garden that is briefly open to visitors during the summer, for the more vigorous walkers with an interest in gardens, the little village of Hidcote over the border in Gloucester, provide an excuse for a slightly longer excursion.

Maps: Pathfinders: 1020 & 1021 or Landranger: 151

Start: St Mary's Parish Church, Ilmington (Map Reference SP 209 434)

Distance: 5 miles

Transport: Infrequent services operate from Moreton and Shipston.

Refreshment: Ilmington has a couple of attractive inns.

Within a walled churchyard at the centre of the village stands the very attractive St Mary's Church, the path to it lined by twelve limes representing the Apostles. The base of an early preaching cross stands to the west of the tower and by the path to the porch door, a tombstone in memory of Hutton Corbit records with precision his longevity at one hundred and six years, nine months and eleven days. Although buried here, his family were Catholic sympathisers and at one time held the manor at nearby Lark Stoke. Close by, another stone depicts the Flight into Egypt and in the south-west corner is the grave of Sam Bennett, whose fiddle sounded the

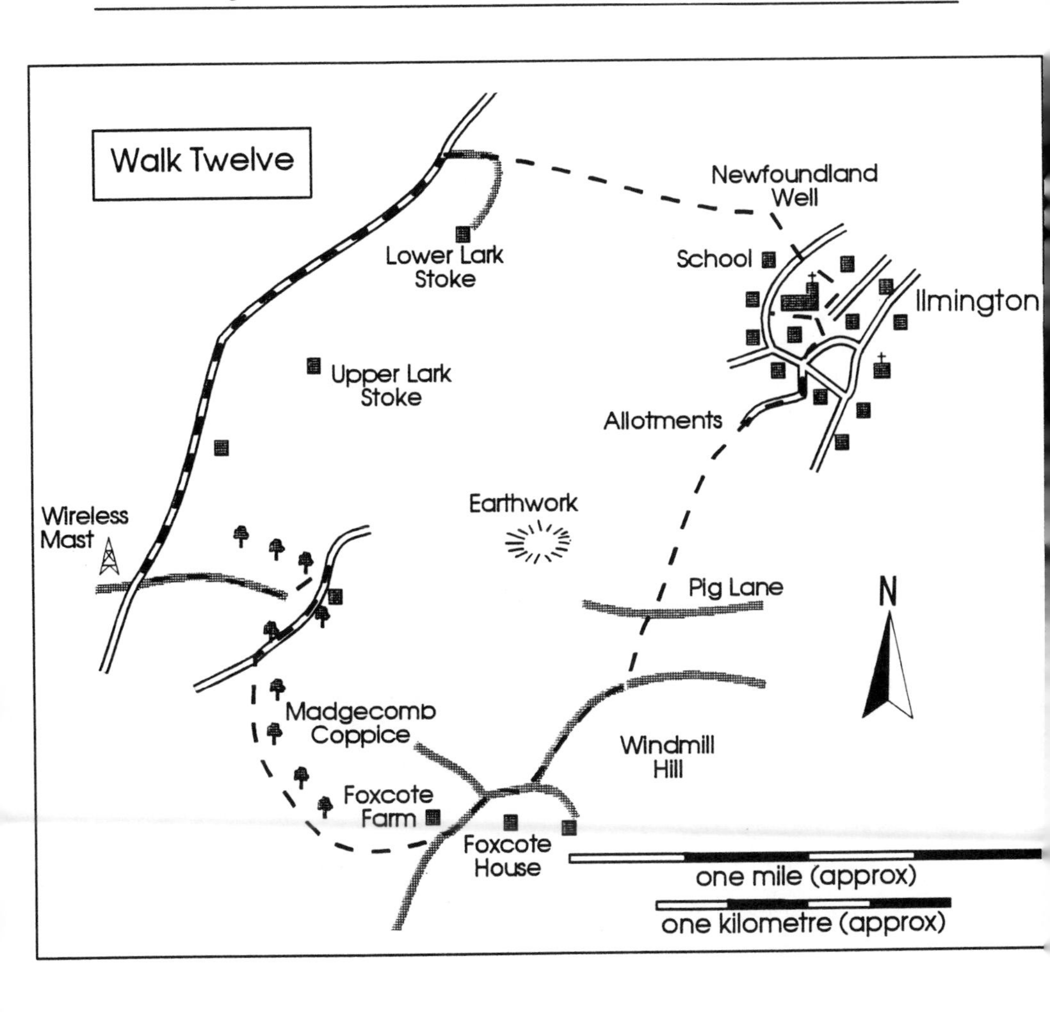

traditional tunes of the village Morrismen until his death in 1951. The bright airiness of the Norman nave is due to the clerestory windows, added with the northern transept in the fourteenth century. Notice the grotesque head carved on its arch, whilst on the arch to the southern transept are carvings thought to represent the parents of Jesus and John the Baptist. Set into the chancel wall are sedilia, seats for priests officiating at mass. Robert Thompson, a Yorkshireman, crafted the beautiful oak furnishings in the 1930s. His pews are decorated with grapes, and the pulpit, flowers and acorns. Discretely carved amongst all the ornamentation are eleven tiny mice, his signature.

Through a gate in the north-eastern corner of the churchyard, a path crosses a meadow by the ancient fish ponds to a road opposite the village school. To the right of the school, another footpath works around its perimeter, where a stile returns you to the fields. With your back to the school, walk across the next couple of meadows, to a reach a third, much longer field. Bearing a little left, keep going towards its top corner. As you approach, look for a stile in the hedge on the right leading to a grass track. Climb up it to the left, passing the strangely named Newfoundland Well.

The spring was discovered in 1684 and the therapeutic properties of its chalybeate waters brought it a short period of fame. The view ahead from the crest is to Meon Hill, standing on the county's western boundary. Not surprisingly, the vantage was the site of an early British camp that covered quite a considerable area. Some strange tales have developed around it, on the eves of Christmas and New Year, a ghostly huntsman is said to ride with his dogs in pursuit of a fox. He had supposedly met his end at the teeth of his own hounds after they failed to recognise him. More tangible, although never resolved, was the murder there of a farm labourer in 1945, who was found with his throat cut and body pinioned to the ground by a pitch-fork. The manner of his death was said to be that traditionally meted out to those suspected of involvement in the black arts, but even the celebrated Fabian of the Yard could throw no light on the case. His assistant returned each anniversary for many years in the hope that the perpetrator might reveal himself.

Eventually the track loses height to a stile, continuing beyond to another. Now in a rough meadow, keep going downhill, crossing the stream at the bottom over a culvert to the left of a small pond. Pass into a field on the far side and climb beside its edge to a gravel drive at Lower Lark Stoke. Turn right and go to the lane at its end. To the left, an old drove road climbs Stoke

Hill, along which expansive retrospective panoramas open for your enjoyment.

The flat crown of the hill robs immediacy from the views from this, the highest point in Warwickshire. However, a short wander to the south and the west will afford different aspects over the surrounding countryside.

Across the fields, near Foxcote

Hidcote with its three fine gardens lies just to the west. At the National Trust gardens of Hidcote Manor you can obtain light meals and snacks and, close by, are the equally attractive gardens at Kiftsgate Court and Vale House at Hidcote Boyce. The clear track west from the transmitter descends into Hidcote and you can then either retrace your steps to return here, or alternatively, skirt the hill to the south by lane and footpath to rejoin the route near Foxcote.

Turn left at the transmitter on a descending track through the fields on the eastern slope of the hill. Initially it follows an overgrown dilapidated stone wall and later, a strip of woodland, at the bottom of which, a path drops through the trees into a small pasture. Walk ahead to its far corner and leave through a gate onto a quiet lane. Turn right, past the private drive to Foxcote Hall and climb to a bend in the road as it emerges from the trees. A field track leaves on the left, heading downwards beside Madgcombe Coppice to the bottom corner of the field, a path then passing through the trees to emerge in a lower field. Follow the boundary to the right and, at the bottom corner, cross into a sloping grass field. Walk down, making for the right-hand end of Foxcote Farm and turn left onto a track past the buildings. After crossing a bridge, the track climbs beside a high hedge concealing Foxcote House, seen earlier as you dropped down the hill.

Foxcote was the home of the Cannings from the fifteenth century until the death of Philip Howard Canning in 1934. A devout Catholic family, they played a considerable part in maintaining the Faith in the area during the Reformation and subsequent period of Catholic persecution. Many of the local gentry suffered both financial and social forfeiture, but somehow, the Cannings maintained their influence and managed to support a mission and priest within their house throughout that period. Following a relaxation of the laws, a public chapel was built here at Foxcote in 1814, which remained in use until the death of Philip Canning. Older residents still remember the Sunday School's popular annual tea-party which, in the 1920s was held on the village green. The present house, built around 1700, replaces an earlier hall. Its many-windowed bays, divided by tall doric columns, create a well proportioned facade that displays both elegance and simplicity. The gardens, with restored fifteenth-century monastic fish ponds and a woodland walk, are briefly opened to the public for a short period in June.

At a junction of tracks beyond the house, fork left along the main drive, eventually leaving the open parkland over a cattlegrid. The continuing track gently rises in a valley below the tree shrouded Windmill Hill which, until the eighteenth century, had been topped by a mill for four hundred years. Where the track shortly bends, leave over a low stile on the left and climb away beside the field perimeter. At the top, cross straight over the lateral track, Pig Lane, to an unfenced meadow opposite.

Pig Lane is a continuation of the track by which you left Stoke Hill. It may have originated as a Roman trackway connecting Ryknild Street with the Fosse Way, its line running for a considerable distance in a straight line across the downs. On the flanks of the hill, a little to the north west, is a square double-moated earthwork that was once considered to be Roman on account of finds of coins and pottery. However, it is now thought more likely to be the enclosing banks of a medieval manor.

An easy downhill stroll returns you to Ilmington, which lies directly ahead. Follow a descending hedge and tree line through a succession of meadows until eventually, you reach a stile on the right below which a plank bridge crosses a stream. Once over, keep going down hill, roughly parallel to the stream. Shortly, pass right of some allotments and go through a gate to join a track entering the village beside the green. Walk on to the main street and turn right. A footpath on the left leads back to the church.

The Catholic church to St Philip stands above the green and was consecrated in 1935 following the closure of the village's chapel at Foxcote. The building had formerly been the village's Catholic school, erected by Philip Howard Canning in 1867 and the attached presbytery was built as the schoolmistress' house. Splendidly converted, its furnishings come from several places. The pews stood as benches in the former chapel at Foxcote, although since 'improved' by the addition of backrests. The east window contains glass designed by the Catholic architect Pugin for the Earl of Gainsborough's private chapel at nearby Chipping Campden, from where the altar also came. Fragments of tesserae from the house in Rome where St John and St Paul were martyred are set in the sanctuary floor, whilst the window above remembers martyrs of the Reformation. On a wooden memorial to Philip Howard, the carving of a small mouse betrays its provenance and provides an unpretentious link between the village's two churches.

The village is home to the Hodgkin family, whose name has been distinguished in history by Mary Hodgkin, née Crowfoot. During her eminent career as a research chemist and crystallographer, she determined the molecular structures of penicillin, insulin and vitamin B_{12} and, in 1964, was awarded the Nobel Prize for chemistry.

Walk 13: Honington, Idlicote and Whatcote

Entering Honington from Shipston, the road passes between the pillars of the estate gateway and crosses the gently flowing Stour by an elegant five-arched seventeenth-century bridge adorned with stone balls. It is suggested that the village's name described a place where honey was produced, a theory that is amply supported by the spring and summer flowers that abound in the surrounding hedgerows and cottage gardens which attract countless bees, busy at their work. The encompassing countryside is one of gently rolling hills, which returns excellent views and a welcome sense of detachment from the busy world for comparatively little effort. This undemanding walk takes advantage of these slopes to link three charming villages that each display a subtle individuality to their characters.

Maps: Pathfinder: 1021 or Landranger: 151

Start: Honington (Map Reference SP 263 424)

Distance: 7½ miles

Transport: An infrequent service connects the villages with Shipston on Stour.

Refreshment: The Royal Oak in the village at Whatcote

From the eleventh century until the Dissolution, the manor at Honington was held by the Benedictine monks of Coventry. It then passed to the Gibbs family and thence, in 1668, to Sir Henry Parker. He rebuilt the bridge, already mentioned, the church and a fine hall for himself, but despite all his investments, the family sold the estate only seventy years later. In true stately style, a lodge and imposing wrought iron gates separate the village from the private park, a drive winding through it to the entrance of the hall. This is a grand affair of brick, its facade adorned with the busts of Roman emperors whose presence implies continuity with a long gone era. Inside, the ceilings and friezes are embellished with extravagant eighteenth-century plasterwork, which even despite the relatively

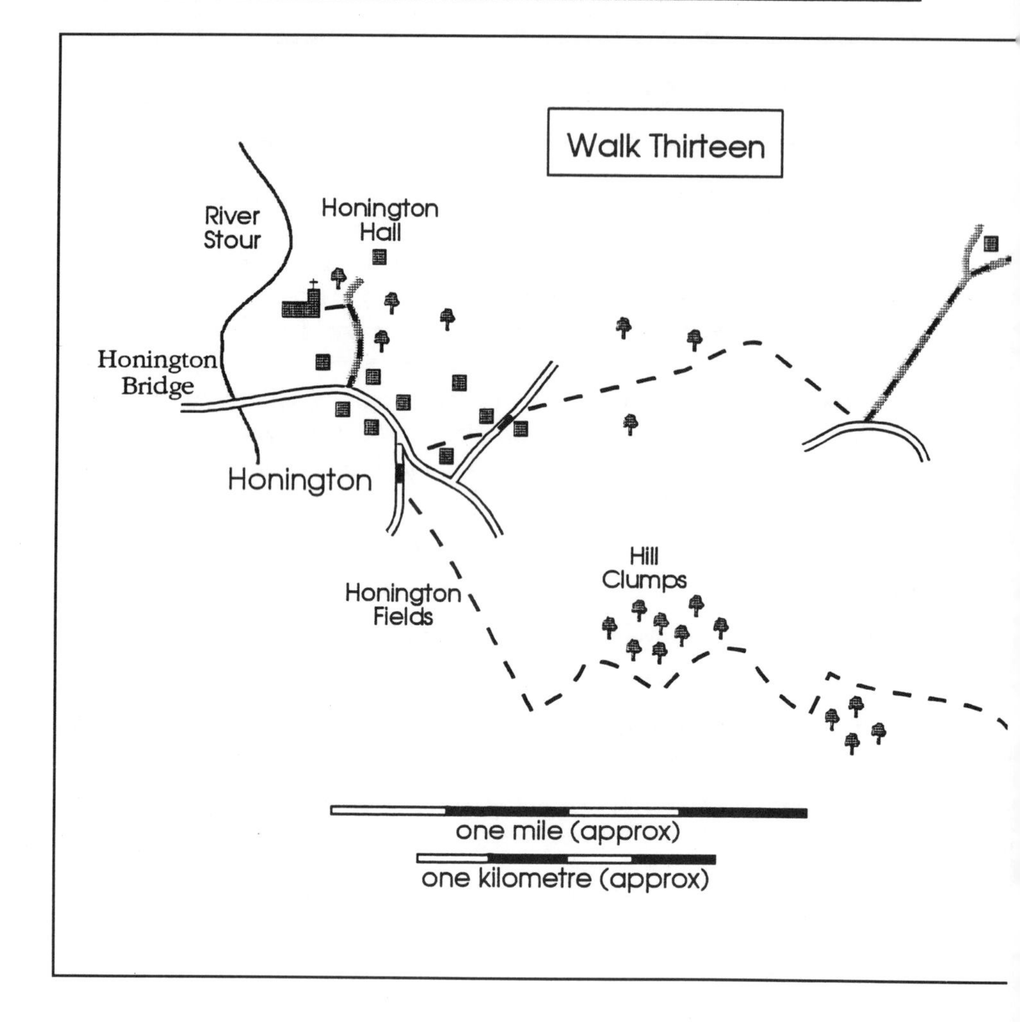

lower craft and labour costs of the day, was a lavish display of wealth. The hall is open to visitors during the summer months.

A drive leading to the church leaves beside the village green, not far from the hall's entrance.

All Saints' Church, entered through a charming lychgate, has a character more reminiscent of the great London churches of the period, although its steeply pitched roof rising behind an urn

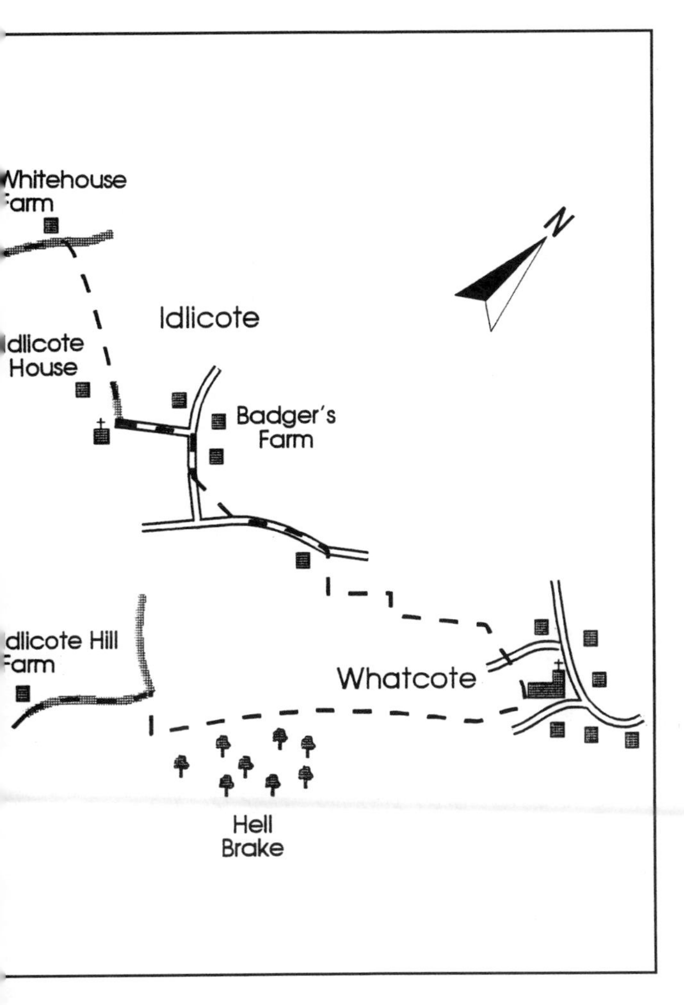

decorated parapet is somewhat incongruous to the Classical style. Such a building is quite unexpected within such a pastoral setting and inside, the furnishings and ornamentation exhibit all the elegance of their day. The simplicity of Tuscan pillars contrast with lavish decoration and monuments, most notable of which are those at the west end and on the southern wall. Henry Parker and his son, in extravagant costume and wig, stand in frozen animation behind the congregation and, on the south wall, arguably the most grotesque cherub ever to grace holy ground embellishes a memorial to Joseph Townsend. In the churchyard, a tomb marks the resting place of Mary Townsend, the founder of the Girls' Friendly Society in 1875.

Return to the village and turn left along the road, walking to a junction. There, leave for a way-marked track on the left beside Victoria Cottage. At the bottom, the path passes the edge of its garden, entering by a gate and leaving

by a stile on the far side. Beyond a small copse is a ridged meadow, walk ahead to a stile in the middle of a row of trees on the far side. A short enclosed path then leads to a lane. Turn left and, at the end of a row of cottages, mount an iron fence on the right into the corner of the large meadow, which serves the village as its cricket field. Make for a fenced gap in the sparse hedge on its northern edge, about one-quarter of the way along. Over the railing, keep the same direction across the next meadow, aiming for a gate to the right of an overgrown hedge diagonally opposite. Now in a cultivated field, walk parallel to the left hedge and pass through a wide gap ahead. Beyond, veer right to an indent in the hedge and again head to the right, making for a gap into the next field near another indented corner. Once through, walk diagonally right to reach a farm track leading to Whitehouse Farm at the point where it leaves the lane to Whatcote. Follow the track towards the farm and go right at the fork before the farm cottages, shortly to reach some barns. Just before the track bends left through a hedge beyond the last barn, leave it and follow the hedge up the field on the right to a waymarked gate. Cross the meadow to a second gate, where a drive then leads past Idlicote House and St James' Church into the hamlet.

Until the Dissolution, the estate was a possession of the Augustine Abbey at Kenilworth. A century later, it had passed to William Underhill, from whose son, also William, Shakespeare bought the since-demolished New Place in Stratford. Shortly after the sale, William junior was poisoned by his son, Fulk, for which crime he was duly executed. The manor house, which lies to the right of the route beyond the stable courtyard, was substantially rebuilt in the nineteenth century. During the last war, it was used as a girls' school, and its light colour rendered it so conspicuous that Luftwaffe navigators used it as a navigational marker on their bombing raids of the Midlands. The isolated octagonal tower to the left of the track is thought to have been removed from the Abbey at Kenilworth, where it might have been used as a dovecote.

All but hidden behind trees, yet giving itself away by hourly chimes from its blue-faced clock, lies the unassuming church of St James. It dates from the twelfth century with rebuilding and additions being undertaken in the thirteenth and seventeenth centuries. Its interior has been aptly described as 'Jane Austen' and admirably demonstrates the demarcations of late eighteenth-century society. The squire's enclosure, its purple upholstery now faded and tattered, stands aloof from the villager's box pews, which stand in subservient regimentation before the rector's grand three-decker canopied pulpit. Another rare survival is part of a Jacobean screen dividing the nave from the chancel. A high balcony overlooks the congregation from the rear of the church, upon which is a small French pedal organ. At the back, protected by glass, are the sprocket wheels and pinions of the restored clock engine, its motive power deriving from stone weights depending from cables.

At the end of the drive by the village pond, turn right. About 200 metres down the lane, go through a waymarked gate on the left. Walk to the bottom far corner of the field, cross a stile into the neighbouring field and go through an adjacent gate onto a lane. Follow it left past some barns, where there is a waymarked stile on the right. Cross and then go through a gate to the left of the barns into a small paddock where, at its top corner, a stile and plank bridge lead to the next field. Go a short distance right along the boundary to a waymark and then turn to cross the middle of the field to a gap in the far hedge. Again turn right to another waymark marking a second field crossing. Through the gap at the far side, walk ahead a few metres to a marker and go right across the culverted Wynyates Brook into the adjacent field.

Some of the fields passed between Idlicote and Whatcote were formerly allotments, a feature of many eighteenth-century villages. With the implementation of the Parliamentary enclosures in the seventeenth century, small areas of land were sometimes allocated to cottagers with no gardens or let as allotments to provide income for the support of the poor. Here, they were worked until a generation ago and one of the older village inhabitants was actually born in the fields, his mother having gone into labour whilst out working. Weighing in at only two pounds, he was brought home in a basket and, despite his fragile start in life, has survived to a ripe age.

Walk on, following the line of power posts to a kissing-gate out of the field. A fenced path passes through another kissing gate onto a lane opposite Old Rectory Cottage behind Whatcote's church.

There has been a church here since Saxon times, however, the present building was started in about 1150. Although it has seen many alterations, it avoided the wave of 'restoration' that swept through Victorian England. A relic of its medieval past stands to the south of the church, a well preserved cross. Unfortunately, its original top has gone, replaced by a cubical eighteenth-century sundial topped with an orb. The church was almost destroyed on the 12th December 1940, when one of six bombs jettisoned by a homeward-bound German aircraft struck the tower. The damage was repaired in 1947, but a new threat comes from subsidence caused by the roots of a nearby old oak. Inside, high in the western gable wall is an apparently pointless small doorway, it possibly once gave access to rooms within the roof space as in many early churches, the priest's living quarters were contained within the church. Behind a blocked doorway beside the chancel arch, a staircase climbed to a former rood gallery, some of the wood from which has recently been discovered supporting the bell carriages. It was probably taken down, as were the majority of those in English churches, in the purges that followed the sixteenth-century Reformation. A monument that provokes reflection is that to John Davenport, who lived to the venerable age of 104, having spent seventy of his years serving the village as rector. Fragments of coloured glass in the south chancel window are from a memorial to William Sanderson Miller, and is the only glass in the church to have survived the bomb blast. He was also a rector here and the last of his family to be squire at Radway. The Saxon font and three interesting seventeenth-century pews with carved ends also escaped serious damage in the explosion, whilst two other pews were a gift from the village's Methodist congregation, when their chapel closed in 1988. That tiny brick building, inaugurated in 1905 when the trustees each laid a brick bearing their initials, stands off the main road nearby, hidden behind a conifer hedge.

The Royal Oak, at the northern end of the village, lays claim to being one of the country's oldest inns, beginning life as a hostel to accommodate the builders of the church. Cromwell stayed there in 1642 and reputedly removed the bread oven from the side of the chimney so that he could look through to watch the movements of the Royalist troops at Edge Hill.

Leave the churchyard by a footpath on its south side, and pass over a couple of waymarked stiles to a paddock. Keep ahead to its bottom corner, where a stile leads to the next field.

Set in the concrete step of the stile are two 'devil's toe nails', fossilised shells of the now extinct gryphaea. It was a distant relative of today's oyster and lived in Jurassic seas between 190 and 38 million years ago. They are quite commonly ploughed up in the fields around here and can often be found.

Keep going beside the right-hand hedge up the fields, gently climbing towards a wood ahead. Just before reaching the wood, go over a stile on the right. Walk beside the edge of the wood to the corner of the field and, remaining within it, turn right. Follow the hedge to the top corner and leave through a gap to a tarmac farm track. Go left along it towards Idlicote Hill Farm.

Just before the farm, fork left on a stone and grass track to a large open field, the perimeter of which is used as a gallop. Turn right and walk a short distance to a shallow corner, there going right again through a wide gap. Walk ahead to join a grass track with a hedge on its left. At the second of two gaps, turn left and cross the edge of a field beside a small wood. Through another gap at the far side, a track to the right climbs up the field. Carry on through another gap, where the gradient levels, to the top of the field at which point the track ahead drops into trees. Instead, turn left, still on a grass track that skirts a small wood, Hill Clumps, and passes a ruinous brick structure and pond. Beyond, follow the track round to the right, coming to a waymark a few metres on. Cross left to the far side of the field and then go right, following its perimeter.

Honington village

Towards the bottom, pass through a gap in the hedge on the left and turn right, shortly reaching the corner. Follow it round and walk downhill to a track running at the bottom of the field, join it to go through a gate on the right. The track follows the edges of three fields, cresting the rise ahead before falling gently to reach Fell Mill Lane, just outside Honington. Turn right and, at the end of the lane, go left to walk back through the centre of the village.

Walk 14: Radway, Ratley and Edge Hill

Amongst the many notable events that have occurred in Warwickshire's history, one of the most conspicuous is the inconclusive Battle of Edge Hill. It occurred on the low plains overlooked by the hill by which name it is remembered. By all accounts, the armies did not have an easy time getting there and that relative isolation, to some extent, still holds true today. Edge Hill is part of a crescent-shaped ridge of hills and escarpment that dissects the country along a line from the south coast to the Humber. To the south-west lie the Cotswold Hills and there are similarities between the two areas, not least in the colour and texture of the stone which is extensively incorporated in the village cottages and churches. The open countryside, which surrounds the high ridge, makes ideal walking country, where distant views alternate with quiet, secluded corners to portray diverse aspects of this most attractive corner of Warwickshire. Although this short walk involves several ascents, they should not prove arduous and are compensated by the panoramas they reveal.

Maps:	Pathfinder: 1021 or Landranger: 151
Start:	Radway Village (SP 371 482)
Distance:	6 miles
Transport:	There are no convenient services.
Refreshment:	There are inns in Ratley and on top of Edge Hill.

Tucked below the flank of the Edge Hill escarpment lies the winsome village of Radway. Charles I's troops passed through here on 23 October 1642. They had grouped at the top of the hill on their way to meet Parliamentary forces in what was to be the first battle of the Civil War, which took place just half a mile to the north-west. Some 20,000 men were gathered in each army and, although the engagement did not begin until the afternoon, it was a bloody affair in which one in ten were killed and countless more maimed and injured. The trial brought no significant advantage to either side, but Charles claimed the day for himself. Tired and hungry, the

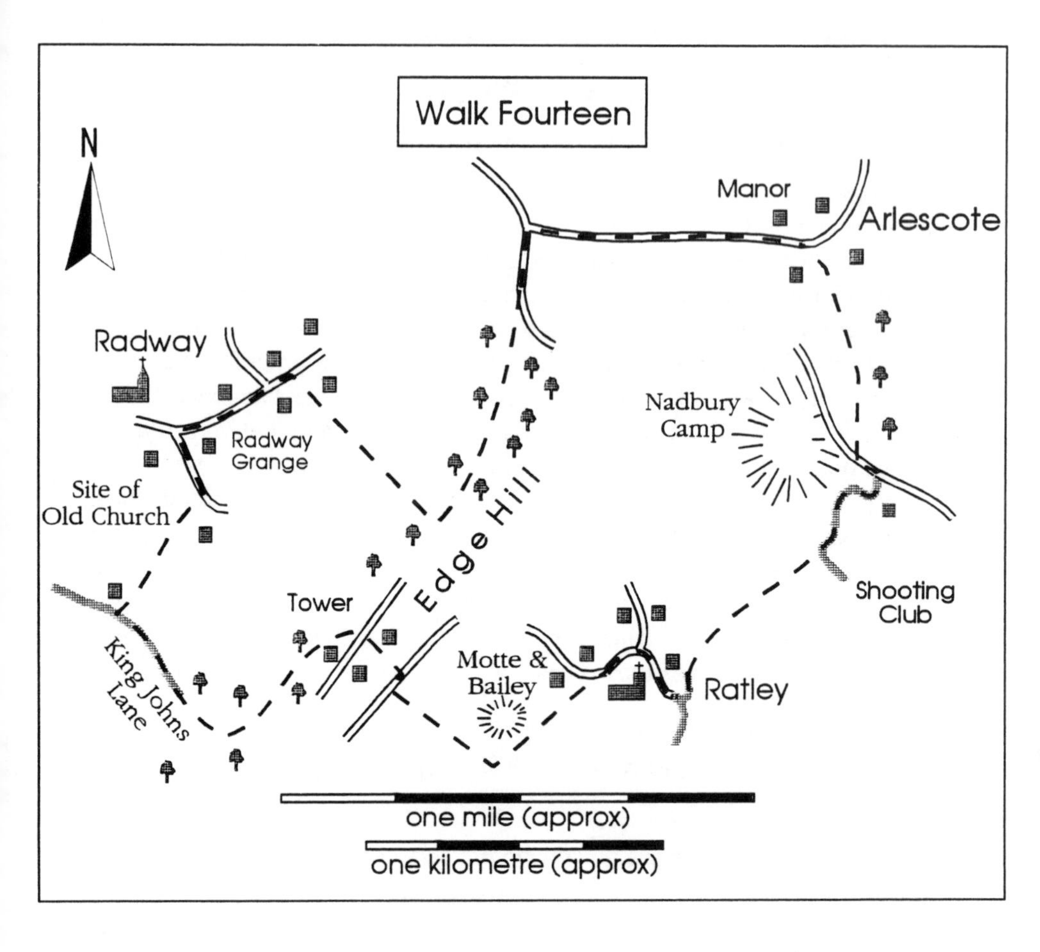

armies spent the following day assessing each other's strength before withdrawing, the King continuing towards London and the Parliamentary forces to Warwick Castle. The country remained divided by civil war for almost twenty years, the strife finally ending with the restoration of the monarchy under Charles II in 1660. It is now hard to imagine the commotion of that day as you wander by picturesque cottages, some retaining their thatch, which gaze out at the world from behind the rampant charm of their rustic gardens.

Radway Grange lies secluded in its grounds near the church. Among its notable inhabitants was John Washington, whose family was related to that of George Washington, America's first president. Another was the eighteenth-century architect and social acolyte, Sanderson Miller. He developed both Gothic and Classical architectural styles and was responsible for much of the contemporary rebuilding work undertaken in village churches and country houses, including the nearby National Trust property of Upton House. Miller made many alterations to the Grange, which he had inherited from his father at the age of 20. He also constructed Radway Tower, which is passed later in the walk.

Near the north-eastern corner of the village, a marked track leaves the road beside Grafton Cottage. Once in the open fields behind the houses, keep going towards trees at the base of Edge Hill ahead of you, where lies a gate into the wood.

As you enter, pause to gaze back beyond the village to the site of the battle. Although there is now little to seen, it is remembered in the names of the woods and farms; Battleton Holt, Battle Farm and Graveground Coppice.

Choose the track on the left, which meanders easily through the trees that cloak the steeply rising bank. You are eventually brought to a clearing, beyond which is a road. Although obviously well used, the later section of track is not a Right of Way and an alternative permissive path runs parallel with it at the head of the fields below the wood.

The belt of woodland follows the edge of the scarp for some 3¾ miles and embraces a rich variety of species within its trees and undergrowth. In occasional clearings, grasses, thistles and other plants more suited to open habitats gain prominence. In summer, these breaks are a wonderful place to look for butterflies, moths and bees, flitting between the flower-heads in search of nectar.

Follow the road down the hill to a junction, where a quiet lane on the right is signed to Arlescote, about two-thirds of a mile away.

Approaching Arlescote, the grazing either side of the lane has not *been ploughed out and remains distinctively ridged, evidence of early medieval farming. The hills seen to the north are the Dassett Hills, a beacon tower prominently marking their northern extremity. The Tudor manor house, on the left as you walk through the hamlet, is a charming building crafted, like the surrounding cottages, from the local mellifluous stone. As children, the future Charles II and his younger brother James, later to become James VII of Scotland and II of England, stayed the night here on the eve of the battle at Edge Hill. Whilst their father was distracted by more important matters, they spent the day at nearby Knowle End, entrusted into the care of William Harvey, who was the king's physician and is remembered for having described the circulation of blood.*

Where the lane bends left past the manor, fork right along a waymarked track. Bear left when it divides a few metres beyond and go through a gate at the end into a small pasture. Through that, the trail follows the base of a sparsely wooded scarp, the continuation of Edge Hill. At first, the way follows an outgrown hedge, but then, at a fork, leaves to take a considerate line up the bank.

The ascending track gives superb views between the trees across the valley to Farnborough and Avon Dassett, the latter's church protruding from the hillside's sylvan cloak.

Ignore the obvious gate, instead follow the top hedge for about another 100 metres to a concealed stile onto the road. Go left, but then leave on the opposite side on a track that winds between farm buildings before dropping into the valley behind. Part way down, the track swings towards Edge Hill Shooting Club, abandon it at that point and press ahead to a fence-stile in the hedge. Pursue the same line to the bottom of the field and cross a diminutive stream. Inevitably, the onward way lies straight up the opposite valley side, the path following the right-hand edge of successive fields to a meadow on the top.

Behind, taking advantage of a jutting promontory overlooking the valley, is one of the largest hillforts in the country, one of several that can be traced along the high ground through the Midlands. The Iron Age site, known as Nadbury Camp, encompasses some 17 acres of flat ground and was defended by twin concentric ramparts separated by an intervening ditch that was still obvious in the last century. The main road, crossed earlier, actually runs in its northern fosse. The site is on private land and little remains to be seen, but weaponry, skeletons, together with pottery and other artifacts have been found during excavations.

Walk beyond a house on your right and quit the fields in favour of a track which descends into the pretty little village of Ratley.

As you lose height, over the valley to the left rise the remains of Ratley's castle. Now, only the earthworks can be seen of what was a Norman fortification, thought to have been built about 1140. Little is known about it, but it appears to have become disused by the thirteenth century.

At the bottom, join a metalled track to walk past the Rose and Crown and then turn left to the village church.

Its dedication to St Peter ad Vincula, 'St Peter in Chains' is an uncommon one and remembers Peter's divine release from imprisonment and impending execution in Jerusalem under Herod. The approach to the lovely building is beside a preaching cross, possibly of the thirteenth century. Its octagonal column still bears traces of carving and is a rarity in its relative completeness. Take care as you enter the church, there are five descending steps immediately behind the door. The building dates from the twelfth century, although the amalgam of architectural fashions indicates that construction progressed sporadically until the tower was finally completed in the late fourteenth century. The differences in style of the nave's north windows suggest that work was interrupted by a shortage of labour and resources during the ravages of the Black Death. Later alterations were made in the sixteenth century, including the construction of the arcade to the south aisle, where a lack of capitals to the pillars and the single column supporting four weighty arches are unusual features. Also interesting is the

Ratley and its 'castle'

marble and stone reredos and amongst the memorials, one refers to the heiress of Simon Bury, who is credited with attaining the grand old age of 1697.

Climb the road through the village.

Despite the changes wrought by time, the village remains attractive. An oddity is the 'First Post Office' dating from 1882, which has an unusual stone letter box set into its wall. In 1932 responsibility for the mail was transferred to the Old Post Office, also now retired, across the road. Glance up to your left as you pass the next building, which was formerly a coach house from which a twice-weekly service ran to Banbury. An interesting frieze of small carvings adorn the dentilation beneath its gutter.

As the road bends beyond the coach house, take the second of two tracks on the left. Marked as a footpath, it leads through Manor Farm to the fields beyond, passing underneath the ramparts of the motte and bailey to a stile. Climb to the far corner of the field from where a grass track follows the hedge-line to the right. It shortly passes Ratley's miniature golf course, formerly one of several quarries producing Hornton stone, and finally ends at a road. A short distance to the right on the opposite side of the road, a footpath begins from a stile beside a drive. Initially elevated above the fields, it leads to the rear of houses at Edge Hill, emerging between them onto the main road.

Radway Tower was built by Sanderson Miller in 1750 on the presumed spot that Charles gathered his army before battle. Conceived as a place in which to entertain his friends, it continues in that tradition as a hostelry, the Castle Inn.

Go left towards the Tower, but before reaching it, turn right onto a footpath that drops down a steep wooded bank to an intersection of tracks. Follow an undulating path left through the wood until, after descending some steps, you meet a track, King John's Lane. To the right, it drops to the foot of the hill and emerges from the wood to then run level. Immediately before the second of two cottages, go through a gate on the right and walk to the bottom of the second field, passing some ruined buildings to a stile hidden

in the hedge beyond, slightly to the left. Go on to the next stile, from which a path leads into Radway, terminating between cottages on a lane.

The meadow on the left, bordered by a row of old gravestones, is the site of Radway's former church, a small affair adorned with a bell turret. It was demolished in 1865, which is surprising since just fifteen years earlier, it had been extensively repaired and enlarged. In the middle of the ground remain two tombs, one is that of a soldier of the Iniskillin Dragoons, recording that his sons died in Ceylon, South Africa and India.

As you emerge onto the lane, notice amongst the buildings behind, a small Primitive Methodist chapel erected in 1866. At the turn of the century, at least fourteen of the surrounding villages had such chapels, but only this and another at Knightcote still hold services. During the eighteenth and nineteenth centuries, Methodism and other non-conformist sects played an important part in village society. Many of the peasants had become alienated from the established church, not because they were opposed to it per se, but rather they resented the power and society it represented. This disillusionment was often focused on the parson, whose duties frequently included magistrate, tithe collector and poor law administrator, and who thus controlled the major aspects of their lives. Sermons used divine support to emphasise the existing social order and rarely addressed the difficulties that the poor faced in everyday life. The chapels, by contrast, provided fellowship and comfort in an informal setting and gave opportunities for the ordinary man to improve himself by training as a preacher or helping in organising facets of village life. Such skills gave people a new confidence in their own abilities and it is significant that many leaders of the early combinations of agricultural workers came from non-conformist backgrounds.

Until 1851, the village also contained a meeting house for the Society of Friends, Oriel Cottage, now a private house. There were several Quaker groups throughout the county, including one in

Arlescote. George Fox, the weaver's son who founded the movement in 1647, was born not far away in Leicestershire at Fenny Drayton.

Follow the lane left and then go right in front of the church, to return to the village centre.

The 'new' Anglican church was consecrated in 1866, utilising some stone from its predecessor, including a couple of gargoyles on the tower. The church is best known for its funerary monument to Sir Henry Kingsmill, who died at Edge Hill fighting beside his king. It portrays his last earthly moments, dressed in the breeches, frock coat and sash that then passed for the military garb of an officer. A window in the south wall has interesting seventeenth-century glasswork depicting the parable of the unjust steward and Isaac receiving food from Jacob whilst Esau is hunting. The panels had been acquired by Miller and were originally intended for Radway Tower. As you leave, notice a tablet in the porch recording a grant towards the building costs, dependant upon seats being freely available to the poor. Until well into the nineteenth century, where one sat in church depended very much on one's position in local society. The squire often had a lavish enclosure, set apart from the rest of the congregation, in fact, Miller had built just such a pew for himself in the old church in 1750. The rest of the village were awarded pews on the basis of descending hierarchy, the poorest being relegated to the very back of the church, often without proper seating.

Walk 15: Little Compton and Long Compton

Little Compton is presently the southern-most village of Warwickshire, but things have not always been thus. Over the centuries it has been claimed by both Oxfordshire and, until 1845, Gloucestershire. Indeed, because of its gift by Edward the Confessor to Deerhurst Priory in Gloucestershire, which was itself a dependency of the Abbey of St Denis near Paris, it was technically a French possession until Henry V's war with France in 1415, when the allegiance was broken. With these many alterations to its provenance, it is perhaps appropriate that the Four Shires Stone lies only a couple of miles to the north west, although even that has suffered a demotion in its status by the bureaucratic changes of 1974. The village's more sizeable namesake has avoided these pseudo peregrinations, although lying only slightly more distant from the county line. The rise of high ground that separates the two villages is perhaps partly responsible for maintaining the relative seclusion that Little Compton now enjoys. There is much to appreciate in the walk including a couple of extensive badger setts, and although a relatively short amble, is well capable of detaining you for the full day.

Maps: Pathfinders: 1044 & 1068 or Landranger: 151

Start: Reed College beside St Denys' Church at Little Compton (Map Reference 261 303)

Distance: 7½ miles

Transport: Walkers using public transport should begin the walk from Long Compton, which can be reached from Stratford or Oxford.

Refreshment: Both Long and Little Compton each have a Red Lion Inn.

Little Compton is enclosed on three sides by steeply rising hills and was at one time referred to as 'Compton in Floribus', the vale of flowers. The surrounding hedgerows and small copses still harbour spring and summer blossoms, but gone are the wild-flower meadows that would have prompted its epithet. Ragstone cottages haphazardly line its lanes and, at one time, it supported shops, smithy and even a brewery. Yet the manor house and church remain at its heart, their gabled roofs barely distinguishable as separate entities.

After the Dissolution, the manor was granted to Thomas Pope, founder of Trinity College in Oxford. His family remained until 1641, when it was sold to Thomas Juxon in 1641. His brother, William, was Bishop of London and close friend and adviser to Charles I. With the approach of civil war, he judiciously resigned his government positions, but retained allegiance to Charles and later attended him at his execution. After, William retired to Little Compton, unable to accept the puritanical liturgy and, although then 67, devoted much time to hunting. On Sundays he walked to nearby Chastleton House, where he conducted divine service for his Loyalist friends. With the restoration of Charles II, William, then 78, was appointed Archbishop of Canterbury and officiated at the 1660 coronation. He died three years later and, although buried in the chapel at St John's College at Oxford, his ghost is claimed to wander the old passages here at the manor house, reciting the once-proscribed Anglican services. A succession of owners followed over the centuries until the house was bought by it present owner, Mr Reed, who has established a business school. Although much altered and added to since its fifteenth-century origins, the house remains a most charming building.

The church was re-dedicated to St Denys (the 'y' being a local spelling) in 1056 on its endowment to Deerhurst. Following a substantial rebuilding in 1863, little remains from the original church other than a few Norman fragments incorporated into the south windows of the chancel. The unusual tower dates to the fourteenth century, its twin-gabled roof being appropriately described as 'saddleback'. That a chapel once existed below the tower can be inferred from a small recess in the east wall marking the altar. The present chapel windows depict St Denis and Charles I who both suffered separation from their heads for their respective causes. Another window containing fragments of glass from the

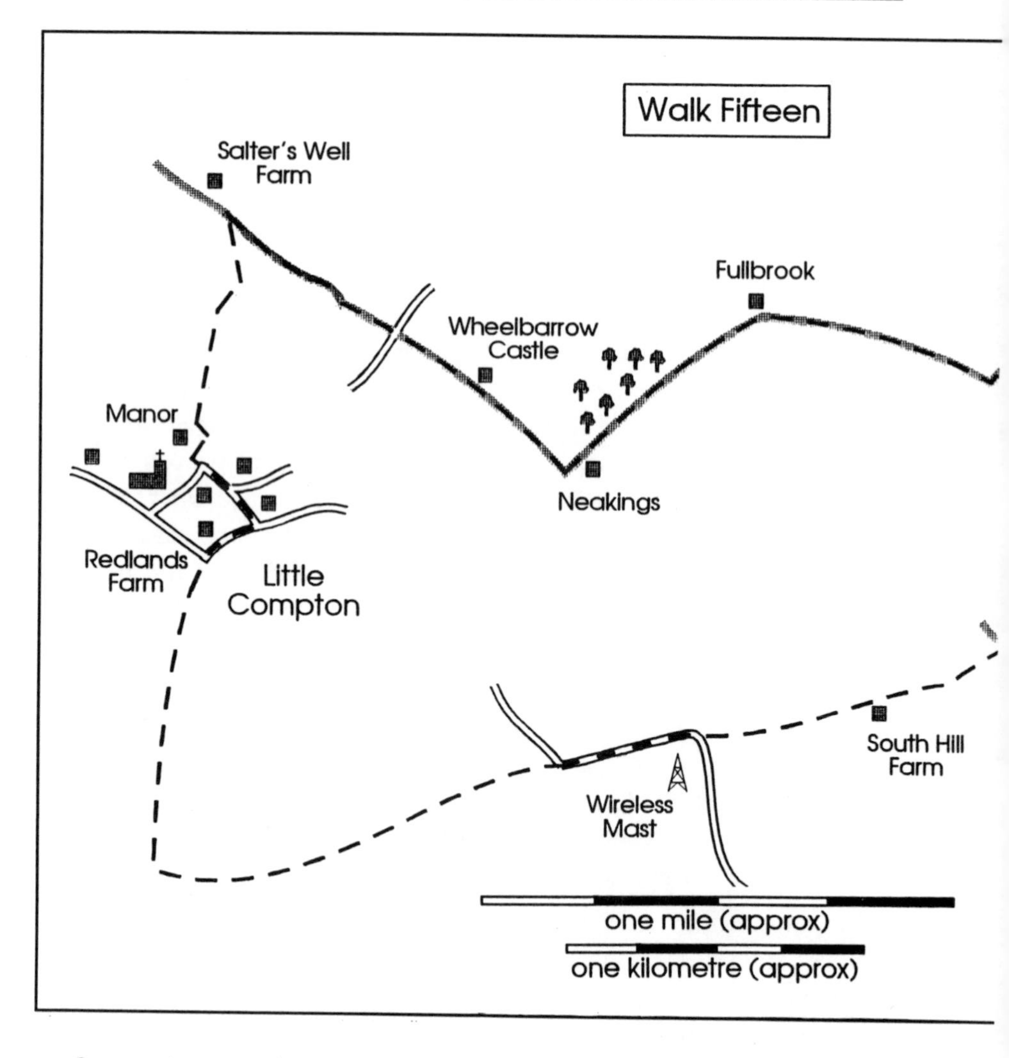

Somme is a touching memorial placed there by Captain Mace, who found them in the ruined church of Villers Bretonneux in 1918. Inset in the nave floor, the tombs of Thomas Juxon and his daughter Elizabeth, are confusing. Their deaths are recorded in 1643 and 1652, although they actually died in 1644 and 1653. Under the Julian calendar, the church's new year was reckoned from the Feast of the Annunciation of the Blessed Virgin, 25 March. With the

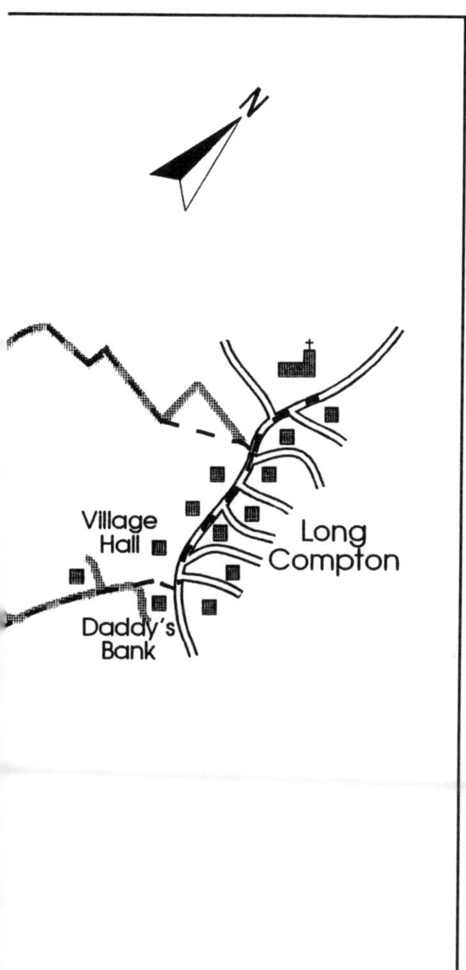

eventual adoption of the Gregorian calendar by Britain in 1752, the year was deemed to begin on 1 January, bringing it into line with much of Europe. Odd echoes of the old calender still remain, one being that the tax year begins on 6 April, equivalent to the old Julian 25 March. When you leave the church, note that the over-carved date on Frederick Harris' tomb by the entrance to the church, this change is simply the result of a stone mason's error.

Leave the road where it bends by the church and go through a small gateway, marked Reed College. Cross a tiny courtyard and, emerging through a hedge, turn away from the manor house and then go left through a wall gate to the stables. Turn right and then left, walking between the stables and barns to a field gate. Immediately beyond, climb a stile into a paddock on the right and walk up to its top far corner. Cross another stile and turn right through a gap into the next field and follow the left-hand hedge to the top. There, ignore the wide gap near its corner, choosing instead a smaller waymarked opening just beyond leading to a patch of uncultivated ground near Salter's Well Farm. Walk across to a track at its far side and turn right. It initially runs as a sunken grass track across the top edge of the field you have just climbed.

Amongst the trees and bushes in the left-hand banking are a number of burrows, the several entrances to a badger sett. Often favouring woodland, badgers are equally at home on the fringes of cultivated areas, seeking cover for their setts below hedges or in small patches of shrubbery. Their principle diet is earthworms, but they are quite catholic and will also eat seeds, berries, fruit and occasionally carrion. Prolific tunnellers, badgers are continually extending their burrows and most inhabited setts will show signs of fresh excavation. Once settled, a cete will inhabit the same burrows for many generations, and some have been shown to be over one hundred years old. Badgers appear to make good neighbours and are known to have taken over rabbit warrens and also accept wandering foxes, who are rather lazy when it comes to digging burrows. Recent mounds of earth, balls of old bracken or grass, latrine pits and foot prints are all signs that a site is active and, if you have the time and patience to spend waiting quietly at a discrete distance downwind after dusk, you may be fortunate to see them come out to feed and play. The best time to look would be in May, when you might also see cubs beginning to explore the outside world.

Shortly, the track rises and eventually crosses a lane. Keep going ahead along a dirt-track and, after passing a barn and then a cottage known as Wheelbarrow Castle, the track crosses the tops of successive fields to more barns at Neakings. Turn left, passing between an open barn and some old cattle sheds and follow a descending track beside woodland. Beyond the trees the track levels, passing more barns at Fullbrook and then continuing across a series of open grazing fields towards Long Compton. Closer to the village, the fields are markedly ridged and furrowed, being sufficiently deep to hide the sheep that now graze these old fields. The way cuts across the corner of the last field, rejoining the track to emerge from the fields onto the main road by the village store.

Straddling the steep valley of Nethercote Brook, Long Compton's history is ancient and shrouded in mystic tales and sorcery. On the hilltop to the south stand the Rollright Stones, a monolithic King Stone with a nearby stone circle and upright slabs from a burial mound. Legend tells that a long-forgotten warrior was accosted there by a witch, who cried 'If Long Compton thou canst see, King of England shalt thou be'. He rushed forward to look at the village, but his view was blocked by the long barrow and steep slope. She immediately cursed him and his men, turning them to stone and herself into an elder tree. One feels there must be some truth in the story for the stones are there to see. Perhaps more believably, they have been ascribed to burial monuments or astronomical markers for an ancient calender. Nevertheless, the spot was a traditional meeting place for Long Compton's witches, of whom it was once said, were sufficient in number to pull a cart up the hill. In 1875, Ann Tennent, one of sixteen poor women believed to be witches, was ritually killed by a farmer, Jems Heywood. She had supposedly turned her evil eye on his cattle and he impaled her to the ground with a wooden pitchfork.

The church lies along the road to the left.

Even this holy building is not without its legend, telling of a miracle performed by Saint Augustine, the first Archbishop of Canterbury.

Lychgate to St Peter & St Paul's church at Long Compton

On a visit to the church, he excommunicated the lord of the manor for refusing to pay tithes. Later, before beginning mass, Augustine proclaimed that no excommunicated person could remain in the church during the celebration, whereupon a dead man rose from his grave and retired outside. After the service, Augustine found him and discovered that he also had been excommunicated for the same offence 150 years earlier, whereupon he raised the dead man's priest who then forgave him. On hearing of the events, the lord also repented, but of what then happened, nothing more is said. Whatever the truth, it lends support to there being a church here from about 450, although the origins of today's building can only be traced to the thirteenth century.

The church, dedicated to the Saints Peter and Paul is approached through a most unusual lychgate, a sixteenth-century stone gatehouse complete with chimney stack and thatched roof. Possibly once a priest's house, it was later a workshop for the village cobbler. The building was restored by a local builder and in 1964, presented to the church gatehouse as a memorial to him. Beyond, a yew-lined path winds to the porch, in which lies a carved tomb slab showing a lady elegantly dressed in fifteenth-century costume and head-dress. A redundant sundial inscribed by the door to the church indicates that the porch post-dates it. Two more can be found outside, one to the east of the porch and the second on the south-east buttress of the chancel. In the lofty nave, twelve corbels below the roof trusses sport interesting carvings of angels and people, some wearing conspicuous head-dresses and one carrying pincers and a hammer, which probably is a representation of St Eloy.

Return south through the village, continuing past the village store and beyond the village hall.

In 1231, the village was granted a licence to hold a weekly market and a three day fair and has remained an industrious place since. In the early years of the twentieth century, William Hutton described Long Compton as being spoilt by 'huge advertisements of things that motorists want or are supposed to want'. He has probably been turned in his grave by the pervasive trivia and gaudiness of today's marketing mania, yet despite these and the busy main road that passes through, it remains an attractive place and a wander down the main street reveals an assortment of attractive houses and old buildings. One cottage lays a rather dubious claim to being the birthplace of Dick Whittington and one cannot fail to notice the rather plain but striking village store and post office, near which is the base of a former cross, now serving use as a water fountain.

Immediately before the entrance to a house called 'Daddy's Bank', turn right on a concrete track and pass through two successive gates to a paddock. Abandon the track and walk forward to the top, carrying on across the subsequent field to a stile. Once over, turn left and then right to join a metalled farm track. Go ahead on a grass track where it shortly bends right and again keep straight on when that also turns, to follow a cleared path climbing to top left-hand corner of the field. Cross a stile through the hedge into a hill-side meadow and bearing left, climb to a gate in its top corner. Through that, follow the hedge on the right towards South Hill Farm, negotiating a stile to pass to the right of the outbuildings into a large open field. Cross to its far side, bearing just right of a radio transmitter mast and emerge through a gap in the hedge to join a lane at a sharp corner.

Walk ahead along it to the next bend, for which short stretch you are actually in Oxfordshire, and leave on the left through a waymarked gate into a large field. A bridlepath follows a dry-stone wall on the right, swapping to its opposite side through a waymarked gap after about 400 metres. Now a more distinct track, the way carries on across successive fields, continuing beyond the wall's end across an open field to a gate. Go through, and immediately turn right onto a contained track that runs steadily downhill towards Little Compton. More badger setts are passed before emerging at the corner of a lane by Redlands Farm. Walk ahead along the lane a short distance and then turn left into the village to return to the church.

Also of Interest:

BEST STAFFORDSHIRE WALKS

Les Lumsdon

Popular author Les Lumsdon has completely revised and up-dated his best selling 'Staffordshire Walks' to produce this new edition. *£6.95*

BEST PUB WALKS IN THE BLACK COUNTRY

Chris Rushton

The Black Country has plenty of countryside to explore just outside Midlands towns, plus miles of waterway walking. *£6.95*

BEST PUB WALKS IN THE COTSWOLDS

Laurence Main

The Cotswolds provide many excellent walking opportunities, plus the chance to discover its unique and characterful pubs. Let Laurence show you around! *£6.95*

GLOUCESTERSHIRE HERITAGE WALKS

John Abbott

Discover local history and industrial heritage in the company of a local expert and entertaining writer - "A wry and humorous observation" BRISTOL OBSERVER. *£6.95*

GLOUCESTERSHIRE WALKS WITH CHILDREN

Juliet Greenwood

The long history of Gloucestershire makes it a particularly interesting county for all the family. Parents can marvel at the opulent remains of Roman villas, whilst children can investigate the ancient burial mounds of our ancestors. The variety of natural features - lush meadows, the banks of the River Severn, woods, canal sides - are a pleasure to walk through, plus they provide flat terrain for the kids. All walks are thoroughly tested by the author's own family. *£6.95*

EXPLORING STRATFORD-UPON-AVON: Historical Strolls around the town centre

John Abbott

An enjoyable way to discover Shakespeare's Stratford - and much more besides. This fascinating and educational book takes you on walks along the river, into Stratford's streets and alleyways, in and out of its quaint inns and other ancient buildings, and to the many museums, gardens and architectural gems. There are also walks outside Stratford to attractions including Ann Hathaway's cottage at Shottery and Mary Arden's house at Wilmcote. *£5.95*